The Study of English Idioms
From a Multidimensional Perspective

陈慧 著

辽宁大学出版社 沈阳
Liaoning University Press

图书在版编目（CIP）数据

多维视角下的英语习语研究＝The Study of English Idioms From a Multidimensional Perspective/陈慧著. --沈阳：辽宁大学出版社，2023.11
ISBN 978-7-5698-1308-1

Ⅰ.①多… Ⅱ.①陈… Ⅲ.①英语－社会习惯语－研究 Ⅳ.①H313.3

中国国家版本馆CIP数据核字（2023）第129611号

多维视角下的英语习语研究
DUOWEI SHIJIAO XIA DE YINGYU XIYU YANJIU

出　版　者：辽宁大学出版社有限责任公司
　　　　　　（地址：沈阳市皇姑区崇山中路66号　　邮政编码：110036）
印　刷　者：鞍山新民进电脑印刷有限公司
发　行　者：辽宁大学出版社有限责任公司
幅面尺寸：145mm×210mm
印　　　张：9.25
字　　　数：280千字
出版时间：2023年11月第1版
印刷时间：2023年11月第1次印刷
责任编辑：李天泽
封面设计：高梦琦
责任校对：田苗妙

书　　　号：ISBN 978-7-5698-1308-1
定　　　价：55.00元

联系电话：024-86864613
邮购热线：024-86830665
网　　址：http://press.lnu.edu.cn

Introduction of the author

CHEN Hui, Associate Professor, School of Foreign Languages, Changshu Institute of Technology; Ph.D. Candidate, Department of Chinese Language and Literature, Xiamen University. Her main research areas include Language & Education, Sociolinguistics, and Computational Linguistics.

She has published nearly 30 papers in domestic and foreign academic journals, among which one was included in CSSCI, three were included in Peking University Core Collection, three were included in EI, six were included in CPCI-SSH, and one was included in SSCI. She has published two monographs, edited three textbooks, and has led or participated in six provincial and ministerial-level research projects, winning one provincial and ministerial-level teaching achievement award.

Some of the core ideas in this work have been published as major papers in core academic journals.

[1] Chen H, & Wu X Z. Chinese Learners' English Idiom Comprehension[C]//International Symposium on Modern Education and Human Sciences (MEHS). Zhangjiajie, 2014: 588-592. Indexed by CPCI-SSH

[2] Chen, H., & Wu, X Z. A Teaching Experiment of Chinese College Students' English Idiom Comprehension[J]. International Journal of Emerging Technologies in Learning, 2017, 6: 22-30. Indexed by EI

Preface

English idioms, as the essence of the English language, carry rich cultural information of English-speaking countries that has been passed down for centuries. Due to their vivid and concise expression, coupled with their close association with specific cultures, English idioms have long been an area of focus for scholars. However, many second language learners are at a stage where they are only familiar with the literal meanings of English idioms but fail to grasp their underlying connotations behind their usage.

Thus, understanding and using English idioms correctly remains a daunting task for learners entering the advanced stages of learning. For this reason, a comprehensive description and study of English idioms is especially worthwhile for scholars to explore from multiple perspectives. In response to this, the author has conducted both theoretical and empirical research on English idioms from various perspectives.

The present study is a comprehensive investigation of English idioms, exploring various aspects of English idioms, including their characteristics, rhetoric, pragmatic analysis, and multidimensional classification. The study also aims to examine English idiom comprehension and acquisition strategies for college students, and to construct several models related to English idiom acquisition. The study provides theoretical and practical guidance for second language learners to comprehend and acquire English idioms.

The study begins with an introduction, in which the background of the research is presented. This chapter also discusses the purposes and significances of the present study, as well as the organization of the book.

Chapter Two is a literature review that provides an overview of trends in English idiom research. This chapter also delves into psycholinguistic research on English idioms and language acquisition research on English idioms.

Chapter Three examines the characteristics of English idioms, including their phonological, structural, semantic, pragmatic, and cultural characteristics. This chapter also discusses the variations of English idioms.

Chapter Four focuses on rhetoric in English idioms. This chapter explores phonological and semantic rhetoric in English idioms, highlighting the figurative language used in these expressions.

Chapter Five presents a pragmatic analysis of English idioms. Theories such as Speech Act Theory, Conversational Implicature Theory and Relevance Theory are applied in analyzing the meanings and functions of idioms in discourse.

Chapter Six offers a multidimensional classification of English idioms, discussing various classification schemes based on syntactic, semantic, pragmatic, and cultural perspectives.

Chapter Seven examines English idiom comprehension for college students from four perspectives: semantic, pragmatic, cultural, and syntactic perspectives. This chapter explores the challenges that students may face in comprehending idioms and provides strategies for improving their comprehension.

Chapter Eight discusses English idiom acquisition strategies for college students. This chapter offers practical tips for students to improve their acquisition of English idioms.

Chapter Nine constructs three models of English idiom acquisition, including the M-E-A-N model, the T-R-A-C-E model, and the S-S-P-C model.

Chapter Ten is devoted to the conclusion of the present study. Beginning with the summary of findings, this concluding chapter puts forward some theoretical and pedagogical implications of the present study. In the end, the last section discusses some limitations and gives some suggestions for future studies.

Overall, this study offers a comprehensive examination of English idioms, providing valuable insights into their characteristics, rhetoric, pragmatic analysis, multidimensional classification, comprehension, and acquisition.

Chen Hui
March 15, 2023

Contents

1 Introduction ·······1
   1.1 Background of the Study ·······1
   1.2 Purposes and Significance of the Study ·······3
   1.3 Organization of the Study ·······3
2 Literature Review ·······6
   2.1 Trends in English Idiom Research ·······9
   2.2 Psycholinguistic Research on English Idioms ·······15
   2.3 Language Acquisition Research on English Idioms ·······28
3 Characteristics of English Idioms ·······39
   3.1 Phonetic Characteristics of English Idioms ·······39
   3.2 Structural Characteristics of English Idioms ·······40
   3.3 Semantic Characteristics of English Idioms ·······41
   3.4 Pragmatic Characteristics of English Idioms ·······44
   3.5 Cultural Characteristics of English Idioms ·······46
   3.6 Variations of English Idioms ·······51
4 The Rhetorical Study of English Idioms ·······53
   4.1 Phonological Rhetoric in English Idioms ·······53
   4.2 Semantic Rhetoric in English Idioms ·······57
5 Pragmatic Analysis of English Idioms ·······73
   5.1 Speech Act Theory and English Idioms ·······73
   5.2 Conversational Implicature Theory and English Idioms ·······81
   5.3 Relevance Theory and English Idioms ·······91

6 Multidimensional Classification of English Idioms ············98
6.1 Classification From the Syntactic Perspective ············99
6.2 Classification From the Semantic Perspective ········122
6.3 Classification From the Pragmatic Perspective ········126
6.4 Classification From the Cultural Perspective ············137

7 English Idiom Comprehension From Four Perspectives ···141
7.1 English Idiom Comprehension From the Syntactic Perspective ···141
7.2 English Idiom Comprehension From the Semantic Perspective···150
7.3 English Idiom Comprehension From the Pragmatic Perspective···164
7.4 English Idiom Comprehension From the Cultural Perspective···178

8 English Idiom Acquisition Strategies ························196
8.1 Current Situation of College Students' Acquisition of English Idioms ···196
8.2 Factors Affecting College Students' Acquisition of English Idioms ···201
8.3 English Idiom Acquisition Strategies for College Students in China···203

9 Model Construction of English Idiom Acquisition ············206
9.1 Construction of M-E-A-N Model of English Idiom Acquisition···207
9.2 Construction of T-R-A-C-E Model of English Idiom Acquisition ···217
9.3 Construction of S-S-P-C Model of English Idiom Acquisition···224

10 Conclusion ··247
    10.1 Summary ··247
    10.2 Theoretical and Pedagogical Implications ················251
    10.3 Limitations and Suggestions for Future Studies ······252

Bibliography ···254
Appendices ···263

1 Introduction

1.1 Background of the Study

As a string of words, an idiom cannot be understood by the simple combination of its constituents' literal meanings at all. An idiom is a kind of prefabricated expression, which has its special meaning, different from a few words' temporary combination. Idioms abound in every language. English native speakers use a great number of idioms in their daily conversation and written language, which has even become a big barrier to those second language learners who fail to be aware of the great importance of English idiom acquisition.

The English idiom *kick the bucket* is a good example. To every second language learners' surprise, *kick the bucket* has very little to do with either kicking or buckets, but means "to die" ! As a conventionalized combination of three words, *kick the bucket* cannot be derived from the combination of literal meanings of its constituents. Not knowing this nature of the idiom, second language learners often try to get its meaning from the combination of literal meanings of its constituents, which proves to be a failure. Of course, at one time the meaning of *kick the bucket* could be deduced from "kick" and "the bucket", or else it would have been expressed by another expression. As Saussure says, language is arbitrary. Nevertheless, language is not random at all. The meaning of a word or an expression must have its origin. "According to *The Oxford English Dictionary*, *bucket* is a term that referred to the beam from which a pig was suspended, by its feet, after it had been slaughtered. Thus came kick the bucket meaning 'to die' " (Timothy Reagan, R. 1987). Most idioms have nothing to do with their constituents because they have changed their meanings due to various reasons throughout the history of their use. *Kick the bucket* is no exception. Understanding and acquiring the special meaning of the idiom *kick the bucket* involves second language learners' adopting several methods.

It is said that there are about 25,000 idioms in the English language which nearly equals to the number of the English words. Therefore, English idiom acquisition plays a very important role for Chinese learners who take English as a second language. Whether a speaker can use English idioms at will in colloquial English or written English shows his proficiency of language. Native speakers' using idioms is a great challenge for Chinese English learners who have remembered lots of individual words, ignorant of the special meanings of the conventionalized idioms.

On one hand, not knowing many idioms, Chinese students are inclined to avoid using suitable idioms when they speak and write English. Instead, they would rather use many unsuitable words which cannot express clearly and concisely what a good idiom means. On the other hand, blind to the principles and methods of English idiom acquisition and teaching, their teachers take a negative attitude towards English idiom teaching, on which very little time is spent. Incapable of grasping English idioms is detrimental to Chinese students' acquiring native English language characterized by concise idioms. Therefore, it is necessary to explore English idioms from a multidimensional perspective and construct suitable models of English idiom comprehension and acquisition for Chinese students on the basis of exploring the rules governing their idiom acquisition.

1.2 Purposes and Significance of the Study

Based on previous studies on English idioms, the present study will examine English idioms from a multidimensional perspective. Besides, the present study will try to develop some English idiom acquisition models and conduct some teaching experiments on college students in China. Specifically speaking, the present study has the following purposes:

1) To study the characteristics of English idioms from a multi-dimensional perspective;

2) To explore the rules or principles governing how Chinese students comprehend and acquire English idioms;

3) To construct suitable idiom acquisition models for Chinese students;

4) To examine whether the idiom acquisition models are feasible and efficient.

Grasping adequate English idioms are vital for Chinese students to acquire English, which can enable them to avoid "Chinglish" and communicate with native speakers more effectively. Hence, by constructing Chinese students' English idiom acquisition models, the present study has great significance.

1.3 Organization of the Study

The book consists of ten chapters. Chapter One is the introduction, which introduces the background of the study, the purposes and significance of the study, and the organization of the book. Chapter Two is a literature review. This chapter reviews previous studies of English idiom comprehension and acquisition. The review includes three sections: trends in English idiom research, psycholinguistic research on English idioms and language acquisition research on English idioms. Based on Chinese English teaching situation about idioms, it identifies problems of previous studies and puts up with rationale of the present study.

In Chapter Three, characteristics of English idioms are discussed from the phonetic characteristics, structural characteristics, semantic characteristics, pragmatic characteristics, cultural characteristics and variations of English idioms.

Chapter Four focuses on rhetoric devices in English idioms. This chapter explores phonological and semantic rhetoric in English idioms, highlighting the figurative language used in English idioms.

Chapter Five presents a pragmatic analysis of English idioms, using theories such as Speech Act Theory, Conversational Implicature Theory and Relevance Theory to analyze the meaning and function of idioms in discourse.

Chapter Six offers a multidimensional classification of English idioms, discussing various classification schemes based on syntactic, semantic, pragmatic, and cultural perspectives.

Chapter Seven examines English idiom comprehension for Chinese students from four perspectives: semantic, pragmatic, cultural, and syntactic perspectives. This chapter explores the challenges that students may face in comprehending idioms and provides strategies for improving their comprehension.

Chapter Eight discusses English idiom acquisition strategies for Chinese students, which offers practical tips for students to improve their acquisition of idiomatic expressions.

Chapter Nine constructs three models of English idiom acquisition, including the M-E-A-N model, the T-R-A-C-E model and the S-S-P-C pattern.

Finally, the book concludes with Chapter Ten, which summarizes the findings of the study and highlights their implications for English language education.

2 Literature Review

Each language has three elements, including pronunciation, vocabulary, and grammar. Used as the building material of language, vocabulary is presented in various ways, such as words, phrases, and idioms. Idioms, as an important part of vocabulary, are the essence of language and can fully reflect the cultural psychology and way of thinking of the nation. The word *idiom* is of Greek origin and basically means "a manifestation of particularity" . Broadly speaking, idioms are phrases that are commonly used together and have a specific form, and their meaning cannot often be inferred from the individual words in the phrase. Idioms usually include phrases, slang, proverbs, aphorisms, allusions, jargon, etc., but idioms have different connotations in different languages. Idioms in different languages vary from each other in their definitions, amount, characteristics, functions, and so on. The definitions of idioms determine the other aspects such as their amount, characteristics and function. Scholars in different countries gave different definitions of idioms. The Chinese language is a long-history language, which boasts of a large amount of vocabulary. The following is a statement about Chinese idioms.

In Chinese lexical system, Chinese idioms are a typical unit. As an individual type in the domain of idioms, most Chinese idioms have some unique qualities. One of the design features of most Chinese idioms on the dimension of form characteristics is the four-character form—the Chinese lexicon provides an exact number of the characters in such a unit. (Zhang et al., 2013)

In the statement, it was recognized that Chinese idioms were composed of four characters, such as *wàn mǎ bēn téng*, *yú gōng yí shān*, *jǐng dǐ zhī wā*. Admittedly, many Chinese idioms consist of four characters. However, Chinese idioms, some having been created thousands of years ago, and others being created now, are a string of words conveying nonliteral meanings in most cases. A string of words of four characters which has both literal meanings and nonliteral meanings is called *chéng yǔ*, which is one kind of Chinese idioms. Besides the four-character form, Chinese idioms include three-character form such as *zhǐ lǎo hǔ*, called *guàn yòng yǔ*, more-character form such as *wài shēng dǎ dēng lóng—zhào jiù*, called *xiē hòu yǔ*. In a word, we think that Chinese idioms include *chéng yǔ*, *guàn yòng yǔ*, *xiē hòu yǔ* and other conventionalized expressions with both literal and nonliteral meanings.

The connotations or definitions of English idioms are different from those of Chinese idioms. Here is a statement of English idioms:

Idioms are usually grouped within a larger class of linguistic expressions termed figurative or nonliteral language. Also included in this class of expressions are metaphor, indirect speech acts, sarcasm, irony, metonymy, and many other linguistic constructions that produce an apparent need for comprehenders to go beyond what is literally stated to apprehend the communicative intent of speakers, and consequently, the "meaning" of utterances. (Titone & Connine, 1999)

From the statement, it is asserted that the essence of idioms is nonliteral language. This definition has grasped the essence of idioms. Admittedly, idioms are conventionalized expressions with figurative or nonliteral meanings, just as what Katz said, "traditionally, idioms have been characterized as linguistic expressions whose meaning cannot be derived from the syntactically driven composition of their constituent meanings" (qtd. in Tabossi Patrizia, Rachelie Fanari & Kinou Wolf, 2005). Any expressions with this characteristic belong to idioms, no matter how many words or characters it is composed of. Therefore, the essence of idioms is figurative or nonliteral meaning. English idioms are "metaphor, indirect speech acts, sarcasm, irony, metonymy, and many other linguistic constructions" (Titone & Connine, 1999).

"*Spill the beans*" is such a typical English idiom, which has double meanings. The literal meaning is to tip out the contents of a jar of beans, and the figurative meaning is to reveal a secret. Moreover, the figurative meaning can hardly be derived from the syntactically driven composition of the two constituents "spill" and "the beans" . "*Put across*" is another example of English idioms, meaning "to explain an idea, belief, etc. in a way that is easy to understand" , which cannot be guessed from the syntactically driven composition of "put" and "across" . Therefore, English idioms in the present study are concerned with reference to figurative constructions, which cannot be understood from its constituents, such as "*spill the beans*" "*put across*" and "*kick the bucket*" .

Scholars have done a lot of research on English idioms, but there is still no complete consensus on their connotations. Language researchers have different opinions. Some scholars advocate that idioms should be limited to idiomatic phrases or phrases; some believe that idioms refer to customary combinations of words, both phrases and sentences; others expand the scope of idioms to include the unique idiomatic use of some words in addition to the various combinations of referring words. *Longman Contemporary English Dictionary* explains idiom as follows:

1) A phrase which means something different from the meanings of the separate words from which it is formed, such as "kick the bucket".

2) The way of expression typical of a person or a group in their use of language.

Linguist Titone & Connine (1999) defines an idiom as a set of figurative or non-literal expressions, such as metaphor, indirect verbal acts, irony, and metaphor. McMordie (1978) in his book *English Idioms and Their Applications* says:

> An idiom is a combination of words that produces a different meaning than when used independently. Most combinations are illogical, and the combination is weird; other idioms are perfectly rule-based and logical in terms of grammar and vocabulary.

This reflects the complexity, diversity and uncertainty of English idioms in terms of type, structure and lexical meaning. Due to the complex diversity of English idioms, scholars study English idioms from the perspectives of semantics, syntax, pragmatics, culture, cognition. Thus, the focus on the characteristics of English idioms varies.

2.1 Trends in English Idiom Research

Idioms play such an important role in the system of language that they have aroused many scholars' curiosity. Beginning in the 1960s, the study of idioms flourished in the 1980s or the 1990s in the western countries. Scholars have conducted in-depth and meticulous research on the classification, characteristics, variation, construction, metaphorical and literal meanings of idioms from the perspectives of functional linguistics, formal linguistics, psycholinguistics, cognitive linguistics, and pragmatics. Based on different theoretical frameworks, they have derived a series of idiom comprehension models applicable to native speakers, such as the Idiom List Hypothesis (Bobrow & Bell, 1973), Lexical Representation Model (Swinney & Cutler, 1979), and Decomposition Processing Model (Gibbs et.al., 1989), etc.

From the perspective of transformational generative grammar, Bruce Fraser (1970) proposed the frozenness hierarchy of idioms, focusing on exploring the transformational potential of idioms. He set up seven levels of idiom fixation from completely free to completely fixed: L6—non-strict; L5—restructuring; L4—extraction; L3—interchange; L2—insertion; L1—attachment; L0—complete fixation. However, it is undeniable that most of the level fixation is based on Fraser's subjective consciousness, and this classification cannot encompass all idioms.

Adam Makkai (1972) divides idioms into lexical and semantic categories, with the main difference being that lexical idioms have communicative functions, such as warnings, requests, evaluations, etc., and lexical idioms are related to fixed pragmatic meanings. For semantic idioms, Makkai focuses on structural changes. He has made useful and in-depth research on the structure of English idioms, and has proposed a precise and systematic standard for classifying and subclassifying idioms with different structures or functions. However,

Makkai's use of the potential mood of false information as a criterion for judging idioms has been questioned, as contextualization can greatly reduce the possibility of false information in emotional or textual conditions.

Jurg Strassler (1982) focused on analyzing the functional use of idioms, and compiled a large amount of idiom data in natural contexts. His research is mainly based on spoken interaction behavior, and he claimed that idioms can only be used in specific social contexts, reflecting the power relations between discourse participants, and pointed out that idioms cannot be used casually.

R.W. Gibbs Jr. and N.P. Nayak (1989) proposed the Decomposition Model, which suggests that idiom meaning can be obtained through decomposition. R.W. Gibbs Jr. et al. later proposed the metaphorical model, which suggests that the metaphorical meaning of idioms is activated by an independent conceptual system in our brain, based on empirical research.

Cristina Cacciari and Sam Glucksberg (1991,1993) proposed the functional typology of idioms based on syntactic analyzability and semantic compositionality, dividing idioms into two categories: analyzable idioms and non-analyzable idioms. Non-analyzable idioms refer to idioms where there is no connection between the components and meaning, and both semantic and syntactic analysis do not apply; analyzable idioms refer to idioms where language analysis results match the idioms' meaning. They further classified idioms into two types: transparent idioms and opaque idioms. This classification suggests how we comprehend and use idioms to some degree, but practical usage of idioms should also take pragmatic factors into account.

Rosamund Moon (1998) realized that it is impossible to classify all idioms into one category and examined idioms from the vocabulary and grammatical level based on corpus linguistics. She focused on the use and fixed expressions of idioms and mainly used the Oxford Hector Pilot Corpus to systematically and thoroughly analyze various important aspects of English expressions, and found that pure idioms are rare and tend to appear in written language. However, Moon's use of corpus linguistics is limited because there are not many spoken language data in the corpus, so the data obtained from the research results are not universally applicable.

Rachel Giora (1999) proposed the graded salience hypothesis, which suggests that salient meanings are always automatically accessed first. Giora suggested that idiom understanding involves two stages: an initial activation phase, followed by a later integration phase. In the first stage, salient meanings are always activated, even if they may not fit the context. In the integration stage, some meanings are retained and contribute to the overall understanding of the idiom, while others are suppressed. The graded salience hypothesis can explain the significant inconsistency in processing literal and non-literal language, due to the differences in processing salient and non-salient meanings, and unfamiliar idioms will entail extra processing.

Chitra Fernando (2000) proposed functionalization of idioms, where she primarily studied the function of idioms in contextual communication rather than their function in phrases and sentences. She believed that one of the main functions of idioms is to assist communication and express people's thoughts effectively. She also applied Halliday's three pure functional theories to idioms, proposing the concept function (ideational idiom), interpersonal function (interpersonal idiom), and relational function (relational idiom). She also studied the function of idioms from the language user's perspective, such as how people use idiomatic language to express their viewpoints, emotions, attitudes, etc. The main function of idioms is to aid communication and shape our thinking. However, she did not explain how the overall metaphorical meaning of idioms can be inferred from the individual meanings of their constituent parts.

Cortazzi & Jin (2001) pointed out that for foreign language learners, the key to acquiring idioms is understanding and mastering different cultural systems. If learners only use their own cultural system to understand the target language culture, the result will inevitably cause a great deal of difference.

Based on a summary of the three main functions of English idioms, Peng Qinghua (2007) conducted a systematic study of English idioms from a pragmatic perspective, arguing that they serve as a means of social interaction, a way to economize effort in communication, a tool for evaluation, a means of contextualization, a mechanism for cultural identification and transmission, and a vehicle for education. To some extent, this provides a new theoretical perspective for the study of English idioms and can effectively help English learners understand and master the essence and cognitive regularities of idioms, enhance their cross-cultural awareness, improve their pragmatic abilities, and ultimately achieve the goal of comprehensive mastery and application of English.

Wang Ying (2007) proposed the Holistic Approach, which is suitable for non-native English speakers to understand idioms. In the process of understanding idioms, five major elements are combined: syntax, semantics, pragmatics, cognition, and social culture. Its main features include: integrating relevant background knowledge and information, forming the basic concepts of idiom constituents, and hypotheses and implications derived from this as a whole; regarding idioms as dynamic conceptual structures generated in practical applications, and emphasizing communicative function, pragmatic value, and cognitive effects of idioms. It also suggests balancing the development of pragmatic ability, imagery expression ability, and social cultural ability in the process of idiom acquisition. The Holistic Approach aims to guide non-native English learners to analyze, infer, associate, and integrate relevant information, internal semantic structures, and external contexts of idioms, in order to achieve accurate understanding of idioms. The Holistic Approach provides theoretical guidance to learners and emphasizes input, but whether learners can effectively learn idioms is not verified by empirical research, and the feasibility and difficulty of implementation are unknown.

Tang Yuling (2007) tested the productive and receptive knowledge of literal idioms, semi-idioms, and pure idioms, which is a classification proposed by Fernando (1996). The results show that learners' receptive knowledge of English idioms is significantly greater than their productive knowledge, and both will decrease as their English proficiency improves but the gap remains. Therefore, it is suggested that teachers should analyze idioms from the perspective of English-Chinese language comparison when teaching, and effectively use mother tongue transfer so that students can master the three types of idioms. She proposed relevant pedagogical implications based on empirical research, which have certain guiding significance, but did not provide specific guidance on how to teach or how students can acquire idioms, nor did she propose specific models for Chinese students to acquire English idioms.

Su Mei (2009), in her master's thesis, used pre-test and post-test methods and personal interviews to find that students have little knowledge related to cultural knowledge of English idioms. She proposed that cultural immersion teaching can promote learners' understanding and learning of idioms, indicating that this method is worth promoting in idiom teaching.

Kate Cain, Andreas et al. (2009) conducted experiments on children aged 7-8 and 9-10, testing their ability to understand idiomatic expressions through semantic analysis and inferential reasoning in context. The results further confirmed Cacciari & Levorato's global elaboration model of metaphoric competence, and showed that even the youngest children could use semantic analysis to infer the meaning of transparent idioms and were sensitive to idiom meanings in context. People of different ages use context to help them understand idioms; the ability to understand new idioms in the absence of context is generally poor; and everyone uses semantic analysis to infer the meaning of idioms in the absence of context. This indicates that the processing abilities of semantics and context have a significant impact on understanding idioms. However, their research objects were native English speakers, and whether it is effective for non-native English speakers remains to be further verified.

The following will elaborate on the research on idioms by major scholars in the fields of psycholinguistics and second language acquisition.

2.2 Psycholinguistic Research on English Idioms

There have been a large number of studies of idioms in the field of psycholinguistics since studies of idioms became one of researchers' focuses. Focusing on idioms representation and comprehension, those psycholinguists put forward several models or hypotheses, such as S. Bobrow & S. Bell's Idiomatic Word List Hypothesis, D. A. Swinney & A. Culver's lexical representation hypothesis, Gibbs, Schweigert, Cacciari & Tabossi's structural hypothesis, Gibbs, Nayak & Cutting's decomposition hypothesis, Titone & Connine's mixed-model hypothesis, and so on.

These models or hypotheses can be reduced to two categories: non-compositional and compositional. Non-compositional view is that "an idiomatic expression has traditionally been defined as a phrase whose intended meaning cannot be derived from the meaning of the individual words that make it up" (Swinney & Cutler, 1979), and compositional view is that "a strict semantic dichotomy between literal and figurative meanings could not adequately account for idiom processing" (Cacciari & Tabossi, 1988; Titone & Cynthia, 1999). "A distinction is generally made between two kinds of idiom: decomposable and non-decomposable expressions" (Sandrine Le Sourn-Bissaoui et al., 2012). "In decomposable idioms, internal modifications only change part of the idiom's meaning, and each component makes its own contribution to the figurative interpretation of the idiom as a whole" (Sprenger & Kempen, 2006).

Concentrating on whether literal meaning or figurative meaning would be first accessed, those scholars with the view of idiom's non-compositional put up with three hypotheses.

S. Bobrow and S. Bell proposed the Idiom List Hypothesis, which suggests that the literal meaning of an idiom is understood before the figurative meaning, and assumes the existence of a special list of idioms in the human brain. When encountering an idiom, the literal meaning is first constructed, and if the literal meaning does not fit the context, the figurative meaning is extracted from the list of idioms. In other words, first, one must deduce the literal meaning of the idiom. Second, test the meaning of the word in context. Finally, if the literal meaning does not make sense, alternative meanings, or non-literal meanings, are sought. For example, the idiom "*zhǐ lǎo hǔ*" in *Chinese* literally refers to a tiger made of paper, and when people see this idiom, they will think of a tiger made of paper. Therefore, the literal meaning of the idiom precedes the figurative meaning. In the sentences "They are themselves a paper tiger, not to mention their stooges" and "All the reactionaries are paper tigers", the idiom "paper tiger" cannot be understood literally as a tiger made of paper. In this context, "paper tiger" is used to metaphorically describe "a person or a group who appears powerful, but is actually weak". Only by understanding the metaphorical meaning can one correctly understand the meaning of the idiom.

D. A. Swinney & A. Culter proposed the Lexical Representation Hypothesis, which suggests that idioms and other words exist directly in the brain. When comprehending idioms, processing of both the literal meanings and metaphor meanings of the idiom occur simultaneously, but because word recognition is typically faster than phrase recognition, the metaphorical meaning of the idiom is usually accessed before the literal meaning.

Gibbs & Schweigert proposed the Direct Access Hypothesis, which suggests that when native speakers encounter an idiom, they directly extract its metaphorical meaning from their mental lexicon. Understanding the metaphorical meaning of idioms is faster than understanding their literal meaning, because the metaphorical meaning of idioms is usually very familiar. However, the direct access hypothesis differs from the view that language comprehension is non-selective. Generally speaking, people cannot prevent the language processing system from processing idioms. For example, if a person notices an idiom, he cannot ignore its meaning. Even if he is explicitly asked to ignore the meaning of the idiom, its meaning will still automatically be accessed.

All three hypotheses are based on the view that idioms are non-compositional. The non-compositional view is the traditional view of idiom comprehension, which mainly studies which meaning of an idiom is accessed first — the literal or metaphorical meaning. They all believe that the meaning of idioms is stored in independent mental idiom word lists, and that idioms themselves lack inherent syntactic or semantic structure. Understanding the meaning of idioms is achieved through direct memory searches in the brain, rather than through language processing. Of course, each hypothesis has its own focus. Firstly, Bobrow and Bell proposed that the literal meaning is accessed first, and only after abandoning the literal meaning can the meaning of the idiom be inferred. Secondly, D. A. Swinney & A. Culter believed that when the literal and metaphorical meanings were simultaneously stimulated, the metaphorical meaning had an advantage in processing because it is fixed and stored in independent, single-word lists. Finally, Gibbs believed that the metaphorical meaning of idioms could also be activated without processing the literal meaning of the idiom. If an idiom can be recognized quickly, language processing may not be necessary. His extensive research shows that, in the right context, the processing of idiomatic meanings is faster than the processing of literal meanings. As research on idiom understanding deepens, researchers have found that none of the three hypotheses can explain the meaning of the components of idioms, why they are also activated and maintained for a long time in the understanding of idiomatic metaphors, and why some idioms have a certain degree of syntactic flexibility. For example, "kick the bucket" has no flexibility; "spill the beans" has flexibility, such as "Jim spilled the beans" and "The beans were spilled by Jim" , which have the same meaning. This has led researchers to have to explain the psychological mechanisms of idiom understanding by regarding them as compositional.

Cacciari & Tabossi proposed the Configuration Hypothesis, which states that in idiomatic comprehension, the literal meaning of the words is also activated. This process immediately produces the literal meaning of the words. To understand idioms metaphorically, one must view the idiom as a special structure. The idiom is identified as a special structure through the idiom key, and it is understood as its metaphorical meaning. Until the structure is identified, only the literal meaning is understood. Therefore, the mental representation of each word in the phrase has only one form, without indicating whether it is the literal meaning or idiomatic meaning. Thus, the Configuration Hypothesis emphasizes the fact that idioms are composed of individual words. Moreover, the theory also explains the syntax of idioms.

Cacciari & Tabossi believed that in predictability, the meaning of idioms will also differ. Without context, idioms with an idiom key before the main structure are recognized earlier than those with an idiom key after. Predictability, proposed by Cacciari & Tabossi, refers to the degree of encountering the meaning of the idiom when only some of the words that make up the idiom are seen. If the idiom has high predictability, we can activate its meaning with only a partial view of the words, such as "in hot water", where the meaning of trouble can be activated by seeing only "in hot". If the idiom has low predictability, we need to see all the words that make up the idiom before its meaning can be activated, such as "clean the air", where we cannot activate the meaning of resolve by seeing only "clear the". Cacciari & Tabossi believed that various factors may accelerate the activation of idiomatic meaning. For example, sentence context is beneficial for understanding idioms and can activate the meaning faster. Incoherence in pragmatics can also provide important clues for idiomatic comprehension. For instance, "kick the bucket" is difficult to guess its meaning alone, but when seen in the sentence "We cried for that old and sick man because he kicked the bucket", we can easily activate its meaning of "death" by seeing "the old and sick man". The Configuration Hypothesis emphasizes the importance of the meaning of individual words in the structure in discourse. First, they play a role in immediate idiomatic comprehension. Second, they interfere with idiomatic flexibility in syntax and vocabulary. Finally, the individual components of idioms play an indirect role in discourse.

Gibbs, Nayak & Cutting proposed the Decomposition Hypothesis. The hypothesis held that idioms do not have a single semantic representation in the mental dictionary and that idioms can be decomposed into their constituent parts. The literal meanings of the components of idioms play an important role in understanding idioms. The ability to process syntax in idioms varies depending on the contribution of the meaning of the constituent parts of idioms to their metaphorical meaning. The greater the meaning of the constituent parts of idioms contributes to their metaphorical meaning, the better the ability to process syntax and perform syntactic transformations. In most cases, the meaning of idioms comes from the meaning of their constituent parts to some extent. The meanings of individual words are actually attributed to the overall metaphorical meaning of idioms. In the process of processing idioms, people try to analyze the expressions of idioms in a decomposable way, and attribute independent meanings of idioms to their constituent parts, which forms an overall metaphorical interpretation of phrases. This implies that the acquisition of idiom meaning depends on its decomposability.

The meaning of the individual words is actually attributed to the overall figurative meaning of the idiom. In the process of processing, people try to analyze the expression of idioms in a decomposable way and attribute the individual idiom meanings to the individual components of the idiom, which forms an overall figurative interpretation of the phrase. This implies that the acquisition of meaning of an idiom depends on its decomposition.

Gibbs (1993) classified idiomatic expressions into three categories: normally decomposable, abnormally decomposable, and non-decomposable. Normally decomposable idioms refer to phrases where the individual words correspond to the meaning of the idiom. The meaning of these phrases can often be inferred from the literal meanings of the individual words. For example, "eat one's words" "break the ice" "lose one's grip" "play with fire" and "miss the boat" all have straightforward literal meanings that relate to the idiomatic meaning.

Abnormally decomposable idioms, on the other hand, consist of figurative language that must be interpreted based on the metaphorical meanings of the individual words. These idioms do not have a direct correlation to their literal meaning and require a deeper understanding of the figurative language. Examples of abnormally decomposable idioms include "cook one's goose" "lay an egg" "line one's pocket" and "make waves".

Non-decomposable idioms are a small set of phrases where the individual words do not correspond to the idiomatic meaning. Rather, the phrase has become conventionally used as a unit, and it cannot be analyzed further to determine the meaning. Examples of non-decomposable idioms include "hit home" "kick the bucket" "knock on wood" and "face the music".

Gibbs et al. found that analyzable idioms are easier to comprehend than unanalyzable ones. Additionally, both analyzable and unanalyzable idioms that can be analyzed are comprehended faster than unanalyzable idioms, which require more time to be understood. Gibbs and Nayak found that the difference in idiomatic flexibility can be attributed to differences in semantic decomposability. Idioms that are easier to decompose exhibit greater flexibility. Internal modifications to decomposable idioms do not disrupt their processing, unlike with non-decomposable idioms. The individual parts of non-decomposable idioms cannot be modified or removed. However, external modifications to the overall meaning of idioms do not affect the processing of either decomposable or non-decomposable idioms.

Titone & Connine proposed the Hybrid model of idiom comprehension hypothesis. They believed that semantic mapping can simultaneously have arbitrariness and combinability, with arbitrariness manifested in the idiomatic usage and automated extraction, and combinability reflected in the decomposability of constituent parts and high semantic transparency. Understanding the metaphorical meaning of indivisible idioms takes longer because the metaphorical meaning has little or no connection to the literal meaning, while understanding the metaphorical meaning of divisible idioms takes less time because the metaphorical and literal meanings are closely related.

These three hypotheses, namely the configuration hypothesis, decompositional hypothesis, and hybrid model of idiom comprehension hypothesis, are all built on the compositional view that the constituent parts of idioms play a crucial role in understanding their metaphorical meanings.

Levorato & Cacciari conducted early research on the understanding of transparent idioms. Transparency or semantic analyzability refers to the degree of consistency between the literal meaning and metaphorical meaning of an idiom. They categorized idioms into transparent, semi-transparent, and opaque. For example, the transparent idiom "*zhǐ lǎo hǔ*" in Chinese can be deduced literally as a seemingly powerful but actually weak thing. In contrast, the opaque idiom "*chǎo yóu yú*" in Chinese has no connection between its literal meaning and the metaphorical meaning of being fired. Their research found that context makes idioms easier to understand, but it did not distinguish whether only semantic analysis or a combination of semantic and contextual analysis was used in the process of understanding idioms.

In order to compare the importance of these two strategies, Levorato & Cacciari conducted an experiment in 1999: a multiple-choice task exploring the comprehension of transparent and opaque idioms with or without context among seven- and nine-year-old children. The results showed that older children had accuracy rates of over 90% in understanding transparent idioms in both presentation conditions (with and without context), and for opaque idioms, accuracy was higher with context but lower without context. For younger children, accuracy rates in understanding both types of idioms increased with the appearance of context. Therefore, Levorato & Cacciari concluded that children understand idioms by using contextual analysis first in early stages and then mastering semantic analysis. However, the experiment did not control the knowledge level of each child. For opaque idioms (semantically indissociable), seven-year-old children had higher accuracy rates than six-year-old children (42% versus 21%), which may be because seven-year-olds had more idiom knowledge. Children with poor comprehension of opaque idioms showed a slight improvement of 7% when context was present, but it was not significant. This suggests that older children understand opaque idioms better than younger children, and the factor of "existing knowledge" is more persuasive than "context use". In other words, children may use existing knowledge more than context in understanding opaque idioms.

The transparency and familiarity of idioms used in Levorato & Cacciari's experiment were judged by adults because it was difficult for children to accurately assess familiarity with idioms. However, in other studies, familiarity levels were assessed by children of different age groups or by children and adults separately, resulting in significant differences in familiarity ratings. Additionally, in some idioms, transparency and familiarity may not be completely independent of each other; thus, they may influence each other. To understand unfamiliar idioms with indiscernible meanings, two text processing strategies can help: semantic analysis (if the idiom is transparent) and inference from context (if context is present).

Levorato & Cacciari (1995, 1999) believed that these two strategies are important in different stages of metaphorical ability development. In their theoretical framework, the global elaboration model, the ability to connect the meaning of an idiom with the context in which it appears is a key factor in acquiring and interpreting idioms and other forms of metaphorical language. As children's language processing strategy shifts from a piece-by-piece style to a whole-text and discourse-level understanding, their comprehension skills also develop, enabling them to realize that the literal sense of an idiom does not correspond to its context. Children's reasoning ability allows them to infer the meaning of idioms based on context. The ability to deduce the metaphorical meaning of an idiom from its constituent parts is a strategy that can be used independently or in combination with contextual analysis, and it can further verify the meaning of an idiom obtained through context analysis. According to the global elaboration model, the difficulty children face in understanding idioms is not only due to difficulties in semantic and syntactic processing of language or a lack of idiom knowledge, but also because their approach to language processing is fragmented. In this framework, the acquisition of idiom meaning is seen as a constructive process. Even if the meaning of an idiom is directly taught to children, they still need to repeatedly encounter the idiom in context to fully understand and use it correctly.

Levorato, Nesi & Cacciari examined the relationship between reading comprehension and idiom understanding in younger children. They compared the ability of seven-and nine-year-old children with varying levels of reading comprehension to select the correct meaning of idioms in context and found that all children had high levels of accuracy, even those with lower reading comprehension. Older children with higher reading comprehension showed almost ceiling effects in their selection accuracy. There may be two reasons for the high accuracy rate: children may be more familiar with these idioms, and the multiple choice task may have helped. The study analyzed children's incorrect selections and revealed qualitative differences between these two groups of children; those with lower reading comprehension tended to choose the literal meaning, indicating their lesser attention to context. Eight months later, a subset of the children was retested, and over half of them showed improvement in both reading comprehension and idiom task performance, which supports the idea that reading comprehension facilitates idiom understanding.

Levorato and colleagues' research indicated a relationship between text processing skills and idiom comprehension, suggesting that idiom comprehension relies on language processing abilities. However, there are still some key issues to be resolved. Firstly, it is difficult to establish a relationship between experimental findings and the comprehension process because children with high and low reading comprehension levels not only use different reading comprehension skills, but also have different levels of accuracy and speed in word recognition. In addition, children with high reading comprehension levels read more difficult texts and have more opportunities to encounter various idioms. Therefore, for children with high reading levels, their good idiom comprehension scores may be due to the fact that they search for the meaning from memory rather than deduce it from context. Comparing idiom comprehension scores in two conditions, with and without context, for the same child undergoing testing can more accurately detect the role of context in idiom comprehension. Secondly, it is only a speculation that children with high reading levels have strong idiom comprehension abilities because of their strong ability to use context. There is still no solid evidence for this. Researchers have not compared children's understanding of opaque idiom (only comprehensible through context) and transparent idiom (comprehensible through context and semantic analysis of its components). If children with poor reading comprehension levels have difficulty understanding idioms because of their poor ability to use context, then their understanding of opaque idioms should be more difficult than their understanding of transparent idioms.

Nippold & Taylor introduced the concept of familiarity in idioms in 1995. Familiarity of idioms refers to the frequency of occurrence of idioms in language. Idioms can be categorized as novel or real idioms based on their familiarity. Children, adolescents, and adults find it easier to understand idioms that are more familiar. In 2002, the language experience hypothesis of figurative development was used to explain the familiarity effect, which suggests that children acquire the meaning of idioms more easily when they are presented in a context. Increasing exposure to idioms in a context alone cannot explain how comprehension of idioms improves. Idiom studies that control for transparency and contextual factors partially reveal the language processing mechanisms that may explain the familiarity effect.

Nippold et al. explored the impact of transparency and familiarity on comprehension of idioms. They used a direct evaluation method to ask participants to rate idioms based on their transparency and familiarity. Nippold and Taylor concluded that transparency and familiarity were moderately correlated ($r=.54$). Obviously, not all opaque idioms are less familiar than transparent idioms. However, interpretation of experimental results would be difficult if idiom knowledge were not controlled. For example, better idiom comprehension in older children could be due to their existing knowledge rather than higher-level language processing skills. Transparent idioms may be better understood because they are more familiar, rather than because a semantic analysis strategy is used for their constituents.

What is the relationship between idiom comprehension and text comprehension? Nippold et al. (2001) found that 12-year-old children with good reading and listening comprehension skills were better at selecting the target meaning of idioms in short story contexts compared to children with poor skills. However, the shared variance between idiom comprehension performance and reading and listening comprehension skills was low, with R2 values of .36 and .30, respectively. Nippold et al. speculated that factors other than reading level, such as transparency, were responsible for the additional variance in idiom comprehension. It is predicted that text comprehension and comprehension of opaque idioms are more closely related, as the meaning of opaque idioms can only be inferred from context, whereas comprehension of transparent idioms can still utilize semantic analysis strategies. Another factor to consider is prior knowledge of idiom meanings, as individuals with higher reading comprehension skills may have a higher familiarity rating for the same idiom compared to those with lower skills. Therefore, individuals with higher reading comprehension skills may not only be better at using language processing strategies to infer the meaning of idioms based on context, but they may also have more prior knowledge of idiom meanings, allowing for retrieval from memory rather than inference.

2.3 Language Acquisition Research on English Idioms

For second language learners, the research on idiom acquisition is mainly reflected in the aspects of idiom processing strategy, avoidance strategy, native language transfer and idiom teaching.

Cooper (1999) studied the processing strategies used by 18 English learners with Japanese, Spanish, Korean, Russian, and Portuguese as their first languages, who had resided in the U.S. for more than five years, when comprehending 20 idioms with context. The 20 commonly used idioms used in the test were from the "American Idiom Dictionary" compiled by Makkai et al., with eight idioms used in formal or written language, eight used in oral language, and the rest being slang. The Think Aloud method was used, requiring participants to orally express the meaning of idioms. The results showed that the processing mode of first language idioms was inappropriate for processing second language idioms. Learners used many strategies when comprehending and processing second language idioms to gradually obtain their meanings. The test results showed that in the process of comprehending L2 idioms, among the eight idiom processing strategies, the three most commonly used strategies were inferring meaning from context, analyzing and discussing idioms, and processing idiom literal meaning. The frequency of strategy use was ranked as follows: inferring meaning from context > analyzing and discussing idioms > processing idiom literal meaning > asking for related information > repeatedly practicing or explaining idioms > using background knowledge >using knowledge of first language idioms > using other strategies. Meanwhile, the strategies used by successful idiom processors are ranked in the same order of frequency as the frequency of strategy usage.

Cooper concluded that second language learners mainly use two strategies to process idioms: preparatory strategies and guessing strategies. Preparatory strategies can deepen learners' understanding of the meanings of idioms and provide time for guessing the meanings of idioms, which includes analyzing and discussing idioms strategy, repeatedly practising or explaining idioms strategy, and asking for related information strategy. Guessing strategies refer to the strategies used by learners when guessing, primarily including inferring meaning from context strategy, idiom literal meaning processing strategy, using background knowledge strategy, using first language idiom knowledge strategy, and using other strategies.

Cooper proposes the following opinions on idiom teaching. Firstly, selecting idioms. In the beginning, teachers should choose idioms that students can easily learn, which are idioms that frequently occur in the target language, idioms that do not have special problems in vocabulary and grammar and idioms with transparent metaphorical meanings. In the initial stage of idiom teaching, the teachers should teach idioms that have corresponding ones in the first language first, then idioms that are similar in the first language, while idioms that are different in the first language are more difficult for second language learners and require more time to practise. Secondly, discussing idioms. Students of all ages do not have a clear concept of metaphorical idioms. Before learning idioms, teachers can explain the relevant knowledge about explicit and implicit metaphors and idioms, and clarify the purpose of idiom teaching. Thirdly, defining idioms. After discussing the concept of metaphor in class, teachers select carefully chosen idioms and give them definitions. The important aspect of defining idioms is that idioms should be learned in context and presented in a paragraph or dialogue. Fourthly, classifying idioms. Idioms can be classified according to themes. Idioms can be grouped according to similar characteristics, so that students can easily remember and learn idioms. Fifthly, drawing what idioms convey. Idioms often convey a specific image, and drawing what idioms convey can effectively show the difference between the literal and metaphorical meanings of idioms. Sixthly, dramatizing idioms. By performing activities, idioms can be expressed in both literal and metaphorical meanings. Seventhly, practise in retelling. Teachers create context and tell stories with many idioms. Students retell the stories and write them down, trying to express these idioms as much as possible. In addition, idioms can also be learned through reading newspapers, taking advantage of mobile phones, playing games, singing, and so on.

Laufer (2000) conducted a test on English idiomatic avoidance among 56 Hebrew-speaking, high-level English major college students to investigate whether idiomatic avoidance is related to the similarity between L1 and L2 idioms. The similarity between L1 and L2 idioms was compared based on three dimensions: concept, form, and distribution, and was divided into four levels for comparison: fully equivalent idioms, partially equivalent idioms, different idioms, and L1 idioms that do not exist in L2. It was found that idiomatic avoidance is related to the similarity between L1 and L2 idioms. Although idioms are an inevitable aspect of language, the degree of similarity between L1 and L2 idioms has different effects on the avoidance strategies of the participants.

The higher the degree of similarity between L1 and L2 idioms, the easier they are for learners to acquire, whereas the idioms that were avoided were those the participants were least familiar with, and those whose meanings and expressions were completely different from the L1 idioms. The most avoided idioms were those that do not exist in L2, followed by partially equivalent idioms. Additionally, idiomatic avoidance was also influenced by the English proficiency level of second language learners.

Irujo (1986) tested 12 highly proficient English learners from Venezuela who had been living in the United States for at least two years as university students. The results showed that the participants were able to infer the meanings of English idioms from their Spanish equivalents, even when there were slight differences in form. Compared to other types of idioms, second language learners were able to produce more similarly related idioms correctly. The higher the learners' second language level was and the closer it was to their first language level, the more they could use their first language knowledge to understand and produce the meanings of second language idioms. In other words, when encountering L1—L2 equivalent idioms, second language learners used positive transfer from their first language to understand and produce the correct idiom. When understanding L1—L2 similar idioms, second language learners were influenced by their first language and experienced negative transfer. L1—L2 similar idioms were more likely to be influenced by their first language and produced negative transfer phenomena than L1—L2 different idioms. Finally, when encountering L1—L2 different idioms, learners had difficulty understanding and producing them correctly. Although high-level learners' acquisition and use of idioms primarily depended on their first language, only when positive transfer occurred and the metaphorical meaning of the idiom was relatively transparent did learners understand idioms better. These studies demonstrate that the first language plays a certain role in learners' understanding of idioms. Learners are influenced by their first language and the transparency of idioms when understanding them.

Irujo proposed several recommendations for idiom teaching: first, avoid idioms that are highly colloquial and consists of some difficult words; second, comparing the literal and metaphorical meanings of idioms in activities can help students realize the unreasonableness of literal meanings and make associations from literal to non-literal meanings. Encouraging idiom production activities can be based on idiomatic entries collected by students or provided by their teacher. Thirdly, selected idioms must be similar in both first and second languages, which can lead to interference.

Frank Boers & Murielle Demecheleer (2001) conducted a study on 78 native French-speaking students, testing their comprehension of unfamiliar English idioms without context clues. Second language learners' comprehension differs from that of native speakers, as they are subject to the influence of both their first and second language cultures when interpreting idioms. They also found that learners rely more on contextual understanding for opaque idioms, while utilizing semantic decomposition strategies for transparent idioms. Additionally, cultural differences between languages were identified as a primary source of comprehension difficulties for language learners. These results suggest that teachers and learners should treat many idioms that can be associated with fixed images as non-arbitrary and pay appropriate attention to the comprehension difficulties caused by cross-language and cross-cultural differences. Boers proposed six stages of idiom learning:

1) If an idiom reflects a metaphor unfamiliar to the learner's first language culture, the teacher should inform the learner of related knowledge in the target language culture.

2) If the learner confuses L1—L2 similar idioms with L1—L2 identical idioms, the teacher should remind the learner not to make such mistakes.

3) Encourage learners to use problem-solving tasks to learn the semantics of idioms. If the imagery of the idiom is low, provide context for learners to deduce its meaning; if the imagery of the idiom is higher, encourage learners to deduce its meaning from the components of the idiom's vocabulary.

4) Support or correct learners' hypotheses. If the learner's deduction about the idiom is correct, provide further guidance for the learner to fully understand the idiom's meaning; if the learner's deduction is incorrect, correct them and tell them the meaning of the idiom.

5) Once the meaning of the idiom is known, activate it for the learner. This stage is about demonstrating the non-arbitrariness of metaphorical expressions. There are many methods that can be used, such as linking idioms to vivid and concrete images; revealing the "logic" of a given idiom; and exploring the etymology of an idiom.

6) If the metaphor of the idiom is more prominent in the target language culture than in the learner's culture, make the learner aware of cross-cultural changes.

The division of six stages provides good advice for teachers to guide idiom learning and for learners to explore idioms, enhancing their awareness of the non-arbitrariness of metaphorical expression, cross-cultural changes, and cross-language differences. The combined effects of these three aspects facilitate learners' continued exploration of idioms.

Wu Xudong (2006) conducted a study involving 132 undergraduate English majors, of which 61 (30 freshmen and 31 seniors) were surveyed for their understanding of idioms with cultural connotations (referred to as Survey 1), and 71 (37 freshmen and 34 seniors) were surveyed for their understanding of idioms with metaphoric meanings (referred to as Survey 2).

The study aimed to address two questions:

1) How does the match between the conceptual basis and linguistic form, as well as the cultural connotations and linguistic form, differ between English and Chinese idioms and how can they be categorized?

2) Does the type of idiom and second language proficiency affect idiom comprehension, and if so, does each factor have its own effect or do they interact?

There are two findings:

1) The conceptual basis/cultural connotations have an impact on idiom comprehension: idioms with matching conceptual basis/cultural connotations and linguistic expression are the easiest to understand, while those with completely different conceptual basis/cultural connotations and similar or dissimilar linguistic expression are the most difficult to understand, and idioms with matching conceptual basis/cultural connotations but different linguistic expression fall in between.

2) The level of second language proficiency also has an impact on idiom comprehension: for idioms categorized by conceptual basis, the correct rates of advanced-level learners are higher than those of intermediate-level learners in all five idiom types, while for idioms categorized by cultural connotations, the correct rates of advanced-level learners are only higher than those of intermediate-level learners for two types of idioms with matching cultural connotations.

Tang Ling (2009) selected 30 freshman and senior students to participate in an idiom comprehension test, and then selected 20 freshman students and 20 senior students to participate in a mental experiment on idiomatic thinking. These students had significantly different levels of English proficiency, ranging from high to medium proficiency. The 20 selected English idioms were categorized into three types: formal, informal, and slang. The main objective was to investigate the impact of language proficiency and idiom type on the use of idiomatic comprehension strategies among Chinese university students.

The results showed that the participants used 12 different strategies in the process of idiom comprehension, with the most commonly used being the context-guessing strategy, and the least commonly used being the imagery-guessing strategy. Furthermore, language proficiency had a significant impact on the use of idiomatic comprehension strategies, with high proficiency learners using more effective strategies compared with their medium proficiency counterparts. Medium proficiency learners tended to focus more on the analysis of the language forms and literal meanings of idioms, while high proficiency learners were better at utilizing the context, related native language knowledge, and the relationship between idiomatic literal and metaphorical meanings to guess the meaning of idioms. Idiom type also had a significant impact on the use of idiom comprehension strategies, with a greater use of strategies for formal and informal idioms than for slang idioms. The specific differences in the use of strategies for the three types of idioms were also significant.

Zhou Ying (2011) conducted a study on the processing of English idioms by 20 English major students, as well as the effects of their English proficiency, familiarity with idioms, and contextual bias towards metaphorical meanings on the processing task. The participants were divided into two groups, each consisting of 10 individuals, representing advanced and low-level English learners. Ten familiar and ten unfamiliar idioms were selected, which were first presented in neutral context sentences. Then, 2-3 sentences were added to form a context biased towards the metaphorical meaning of the idiom. For each idiom, two target words were designed, one related to the metaphorical meaning and the other to the literal meaning. The participants were then asked to complete the word in each sentence.

The study focused on four main questions:

1) Which meaning (literal or metaphorical) do learners process first when processing idioms?

2) Does contextual bias affect the processing of literal and metaphorical meanings of idioms?

3) Does learners' English proficiency affect the processing of literal and metaphorical meanings of idioms?

4) Does familiarity with idioms affect the processing of literal and metaphorical meanings of idioms?

The experimental results indicate that:

1) When processing familiar idioms both in neutral and metaphorical contexts, advanced and low-level learners process the metaphorical meaning directly; When processing unfamiliar idioms in neutral contexts, both groups tend to process the literal meaning first; when in a context biased towards metaphorical meanings, advanced learners tend to process the metaphorical meaning directly, while low-level learners process the literal meaning first.

2) Learners' English proficiency has no effect on the processing of familiar idioms, but affects the processing of unfamiliar idioms.

3) Contextual bias has no effect on the processing of familiar idioms for learners at different proficiency levels, but does affect the processing of unfamiliar idioms for advanced English learners.

4) The effects of English proficiency and contextual bias on learners' idiom processing depend on the familiarity of the idiom. Familiarity is a key factor that affects learners' idiom processing.

Among a lot of research on English idioms in the western countries, research in the field of psycholinguistics have made the most achievements, which focuses on native speakers, especially young children's comprehension and production of idioms from the perspective of psycholinguistics. The few research in the field of second language acquisition in the western countries mainly chooses Spanish, German native speakers as subjects. Spanish, German and other western languages are languages that are closely related languages, and there are probably differences between those subjects and English learners in China when understanding and acquiring English idioms, because the Chinese language belongs to Han-Tibet languages. Research on English idioms conducted by Chinese scholars mainly focus on idioms' structures, meanings, usages, origins, and so on, and few research are concerned with learners' acquiring English idioms.

On the one hand, as an integral part of the English language, English idioms are very important for Chinese students' grasping English; on the other hand, English idioms are neglected by both students and teachers in China. However, previous studies at home and abroad have not solved how Chinese students efficiently acquire English idioms.

The present study will try to explore English idioms from different perspectives and construct some models of English idiom acquisition, which will promote Chinese students' grasping English idioms and break the bottleneck of improving their English.

3 Characteristics of English Idioms

To understand and master English idioms, we first need to understand the characteristics of English idioms. What are the characterizations of idioms? This is an interesting question. Idioms as multiword expressions are lexicalized:

> They have the semantic unity of single words but the grammatical flexibility, though in varying degrees, of phrases, semi-clauses, and clauses, which indeed the majority are. (Fernando, 2000, p. 74)

In other words, an idiom composed of more than a single word functions as a semantic unit like a single word. Regarding the characteristics of English idioms, Chinese scholar Wang Rongpei (2000) proposed three basic characteristics of English idioms, namely long-term habitual use, fixed structure, and semantic integrity. This chapter further explores the characteristics of English idioms from the aspects of phonetic features, structural features, semantic features, pragmatic features, cultural features, and idiom variations.

3.1 Phonetic Characteristics of English Idioms

The use of idioms can help people express personal thoughts and feelings accurately, distinctly, vividly, and concisely, enhancing the appeal and persuasiveness of language. One of the most typical features is to enhance the beauty and coordinate the rhythm through the sound and rhyme of speech. By use of alliteration, some English idioms can enhance their beauty and the sound effect. For example, *fall flat, tit and tat, then and there, as mute as mice, care killed the cat, as green as grass, bag and baggage*, etc. Some English idioms rhyme with endings, which means that the main morphemes of English idioms have the same endings, harmonious rhythms, and coordinated phonology, making people read or sound catchy. For example, *art and part, high and dry, as you sow, you shall mow, Well begun is half done* and so on. There are also some English idioms, by use of onomatopoeia, form vivid, colorful idioms together with other words. For example, *bang oneself again, hum and ha, go snap*, etc.

3.2 Structural Characteristics of English Idioms

3.2.1 The Fixity

The fixity of the structure of English idioms generally refers to the fact that the various components of an idiom cannot be changed or substituted arbitrarily. For example, "have an axe to grind" cannot be replaced with "have a chopper to grind" "as cool as a cucumber" cannot be replaced with "as cool as a potato/watermelon" and "eat humble pie" cannot be replaced with "eat a humble pie" . Similarly, "in a family way" cannot be changed to "in the family way", which means "pregnant". However, the fixity of idiom structure is not absolute but rather relative, and the degree of fixity varies depending on the idiom. English idioms can be divided into three categories based on the degree of fixity: unfixed, semi-fixed, and fixed. Some idioms are unfixed and can be combined with various words to form meaningful phrases, such as "run a school/business/company" or "blue film/

story/joke/gag". Semi-fixed idioms can only be combined with a few specific words, such as "harbor doubt/certainty" or "try/do one's best". Fixed idioms cannot be changed in any way and must be used exactly as they were originally formed, such as "bear in mind", "at short notice", "tell the truth" and "lay a foundation".

3.2.2 The Diversity of Form

Generally speaking, idioms are composed of two or more words or characters arranged linearly, but a small number of scholars such as Hockett (1958) and Fraser (1970) argue that a single word can also be an idiom, such as smog, sitcom, Globish, and rats. English idioms exist in various forms, including individual words, idiomatic phrases like "fly into a rage" or "burn daylight", slang like "kick the bucket" or "fifty-fifty", proverbs like "A friend in need is a friend indeed" or "It's no use crying over spilled milk", allusions like "rain cats and dogs", paired words like "bread and butter" or "hustle and bustle", and incomplete sentences like "what about..." and so on.

3.2.3 The Grammatical Irregularity

Idioms are an established form of expression that has been distilled from long-term practical experience and is still used today. Examples include "diamond cut diamond" and "like cures like", and so on. These English idioms do not follow conventional grammar rules and are irregular, making them difficult to analyze using typical grammar analysis methods.

3.3 Semantic Characteristics of English Idioms

3.3.1 The Wholeness of Semantic Meaning

The wholeness of semantic meaning in English idioms refers to the fact that the semantic meaning of an English idiom is a complete and indivisible whole. In other words, the semantic meaning of an English idiom is not simply the sum of the meanings of its component words. To understand an idiom, we cannot rely on the meanings of the individual words that make it up, otherwise we may make mistakes in interpreting the idiom. For example, "show the white feather" does not mean "display white feathers", but rather "to be cowardly". "Bring down the house" does not mean "to demolish a building", but rather "to receive loud applause from the audience". "Play to the gallery" does not mean "to perform in a corridor", but rather "to seek approval from the audience". "The man in the street" does not refer to "people on the street", but rather "ordinary people". These idioms cannot be deduced from the meanings of the individual words in the phrase. The wholeness of semantic meaning in idioms is a common characteristic for all idioms, and is an important basis for differentiating between fixed word combinations and idioms.

3.3.2 The Figurative Nature

The figurative nature of English idioms is the main semantic feature of idioms. Idioms are composed of two or more words, and the meaning is often not a combination of the meaning of each word, but the specific event described by the combination of words, the imagery that it evokes, and the rhetorical effect it produces. Through people's cognitive processing such as deduction, analogy, allusion, metaphor, metonymy and synecdoche, the figurative meaning is deduced, which often contains metaphorical meanings that are significant. For example, "wash one's dirty linen in public" literally means "to wash dirty clothes in public", and "even Homer sometimes nods" means that even the wisest will make mistakes. Because of the vivid and imaginative nature of the figurative language used, we can easily understand its true meaning by thinking through the associations made. Another example is "as poor as a church mouse", which literally means "as poor as a mouse in a church", and we can imagine that there is no food for mice in a church, so the mouse in the church is poor and has nothing. Therefore, the true meaning of this idiom is "very poor, without a penny". These idioms belong to well-founded idioms because they are based on distinct images which evoke associations to their meanings. However, there are also some unfounded idioms, such as "spill the beans" (to reveal secrets) and "a wet blanket" (a person who spoils fun), which are difficult to understand their meanings from their literal meanings. For these idioms, they are unfounded and cannot be logically explained.

3.3.3 The Specificity

The semantics of English idioms, in addition to being holistic and metaphorical, also have specificity. Researchers have used words such as peculiar, irregular, anomalous, illogical, odd, and grotesque to describe them. The specificity of English idioms is mainly manifested in two aspects: illogical and un-analogous.

1) Illogical: Some idioms in English are clearly out of line with logical thinking both in their collocation and semantic expression. They are extremely irregular but have been following their usage for many years, becoming fixed expressions. For example, "face the music" (to accept blame or criticism, to pay the price), "leg forward" (to go all out), "smell a rat" (to be suspicious), "Handsome is that/as handsome does" (behavior is the true measure of beauty), and so on. These idioms not only have illogical collocations, but their semantic meaning is also far from their literal meaning, with no inherent connection. In daily communication, there are also many illogical idioms, such as "You said

it/You can say that again" (I totally agree), "What's cooking?" (What's happening?), "You're all wet" (You're completely wrong!), "Here's mud in your eye!" (Cheers!). These illogical idioms are often difficult for non-native learners to understand. When encountering such idioms, learners should diligently consult a dictionary and never guess the meaning based solely on the words.

2) Un-analogous: The semantics of idioms are often generated by various historical, social, and other reasons, rather than logical reasoning. Therefore, they generally cannot be changed, created, or interpreted freely through analogy, otherwise, understanding or expression errors may occur. For example, "the last words" (last words) and "the last word" (final conclusion) cannot be easily replaced in context because they express vastly different meanings. Likewise, "let one's hair down" and "keep one's hair on" seem to be antonyms literally, but in actuality, the former means "to be informal" and the latter means "not to lose one's temper", they are apparently opposite but have no comparison relationship. Additionally, "upside down" cannot be analogized to "downside up" (messy), and "take in hand" cannot be changed to "take in hands" or "take hands", and so on.

As can be seen from the above examples, we cannot use analogical methods to deduce the unknown meaning of idioms, nor can we create new idioms freely based on known meanings of idioms.

3.4 Pragmatic Characteristics of English Idioms

Chinese scholar Peng Qinghua (2007) conducted research on English idioms from a pragmatic perspective and concluded that they have a rich variety of cultural characteristics, which leads to idioms playing diverse "roles" or multiple pragmatic functions in actual usage.

3 Characteristics of English Idioms

The pragmatic features of English idioms mainly manifest in the following aspects:

Firstly, English idioms have both literal and figurative meanings, and thus the usage and understanding of idioms are constrained by the context. The meaning expressed by idioms varies in different contexts. Therefore, language users need to fully understand idioms based on the context. For example, the idiom "get to" can express different meanings in different contexts.

1) It was high time for him to be getting to work with again. (begin to do sth.)

2) Lily wanted to go to the beach Saturday, but it rained and they didn't get to. (do it)

3) At last they got to their new home. (reach)

4) This music really gets to you. (have an impact on...)

5) Where has that letter got to? (Where? / Where did it go?)

Above, we have listed the different meanings of "get to" in various contexts. Only the sentence in example 3) expresses the basic meaning of "get to". To truly appreciate and understand the nuances of this idiom in other examples, it is necessary to understand the specific context in which it is used.

Secondly, English idioms are concise, lively, and imbued with strong rhetorical flair. For example,

6) A man is as old as he feels. (Meaning: The old man himself whether he is old or not.) Simile

7) Get something off one's chest. (Meaning: Spit it out and tell the pent-up unhappiness in your heart.) Metaphor

8) What is learned in the cradle is carried to the grave. (Meaning: What I learned as a child will never be forgotten.) Metonymy

9) Time tries friends as fire tries gold. (Meaning: Time tests friends, just as fire tests gold.) Personification

10) Hatred blasts the crop on the land; envy the fish in the sea. (Meaning: Hatred can destroy crops on the ground, and jealousy can kill fish in the sea.) Hyperbole

11) My grandfather had gone to heaven. (Meaning: My grandfather passed away.) Euphemism

12) More haste, less speed. (Meaning: Haste makes waste.) Antithesis

13) Like cures like. (Meaning: Fighting poison with poison.) Repetition

Finally, English idioms have communicative characteristics. In the process of verbal communication, English idioms are often used to implement verbal actions such as suggestion, advice, wishes, commands, thanks, congratulations, emotions, attitudes, determination, threats, curses, etc. For example:

14) I won't take no for an answer. (Meaning: I'm going to stick with it.)

15) Don't air your dirty linen in public. (Meaning: One should not shake off the embarrassing thing in front of the public.)

16) Go and chase yourself! (Meaning: Don't bother me!)

17) My name's Walker! (Meaning: I'm leaving.)

18) Be your age! (Meaning: Do things like adults, with your brain.)

19) Less is more. (Meaning: To be brief.)

3.5 Cultural Characteristics of English Idioms

Language is a cultural phenomenon, and idioms are the most

culturally significant part of a language. English idioms represent the essence of the English language culture, reflecting its development and evolution, and exhibiting clear cultural characteristics. The cultural features of English idioms are mainly manifested in their worldwide, national, and regional characteristics.

3.5.1 The Global Characteristic

Although different ethnic groups have different languages and cultures, they all live on the same planet, and people not only share the same life experiences and knowledge, but also possess the same logical thinking ability, aesthetic taste, and life philosophy.

For example, idioms such as "in the same boat" "the early bird catches the worm", and "a near neighbor is better than a distant cousin" illustrate the global cultural features of English idioms. Because humans have similar lifestyles, thoughts, and emotions, different ethnic groups have many similarities in observing things and expressing their thoughts and feelings, sometimes even by coincidence. For instance, the idiom "burn one's boats/bridges" and *"pò fǔ chén zhōu"*, which originated from the military, reflects the determination of soldiers to fight to the death. The former comes from the ancient Roman Emperor Caesar's burning of his fleet to encourage his soldiers to fight, and the latter comes from the courage and determination of Chinese warlord Xiang Yu in resisting the Qin army.

3.5.2 The Ethnic Characteristics

During the long process of historical evolution, people from different ethnic groups living in different cultural backgrounds have formed different ways of thinking and attitudes towards life, which makes English idioms deeply rooted with ethnic characteristics.

Firstly, influenced by traditional culture, English idioms are mainly derived from ancient Greek mythology, Aesop's fables, ancient Roman legends, biblical references, religious beliefs, and cultural classics. For example, "to rest on one's laurels", in which "laurel" is an ornamental evergreen tree, which refers to a "laurel" woven from laurel leaves. According to Greek and Roman mythology, the sun god Apollo's lover, Daphne, was turned into a laurel tree by her father, the river god. From that moment on, whenever Apollo saw a laurel tree, he would be reminded of his lost love and became infatuated with it. Therefore, ancient Greece retained a tradition, that the winner of a sports competition would be awarded a "laurel crown" to show respect to Apollo. This custom gradually spread throughout Europe, and laurels became a symbol of victory, success and distinction.

"Procrustean bed" is a proverb derived mainly from Procrustes, who was the son of the sea god, Poseidon, and a giant who specialized in robbing people. After robbing travelers, Procrustes would cut off or stretch their limbs to fit a bed's length he designed, causing them immense suffering. Therefore, Procrustes became known as "the iron bed thief." Later, the famous Greek hero Theseus encountered the "iron bed thief" on his way to Athens to find his father and defeated the bandit. Theseus used the same tactics as his enemy and forced the burly Procrustes to lie on a short bed and chopped off his legs sticking out of the bed except for one. Therefore, the adjective Procrustean means to "force conformity at all costs". Laurel and Procrustean both come from Greek mythology, these idioms can clearly reflect the ethnic cultural characteristics.

Furthermore, religion, as an important component of human thought and culture, is a cultural phenomenon. English idioms closely related to culture can reflect the influence of religion on language. For example, the idiom "the salt of the earth" comes from the book of Matthew in the New Testament. Jesus said to his disciples, "You are the salt of the earth: but if salt has lost its taste, how can its saltness be restored?" Jesus compared his disciples to the "salt of the earth". Here "salt" refers to "core strength". The idiom "cross one's fingers" is a phrase related to Christianity. The cross is an important symbol of Christianity and the place where Jesus Christ suffered. Christians draw the sign of the cross on their chest when praying to show respect for the Lord. Later, the cross gradually became a symbol of driving out evil and blessing good deeds. However, what if they do not have a cross with them to ward off disasters and difficulties? An effective way is to "cross one's fingers", which means folding your fingers onto your index finger, crossing them to form an X-shape, thus achieving the effects of repelling evil and blessing. Nowadays, people often use "cross one's fingers" to pray for good luck. Christianity and the Bible have a subtle influence on English and fully reflect the ethnic characteristics of English idioms.

Finally, ethnic customs and habits are also fully reflected in the ethnic characteristics of English idioms. As an important component of ethnic culture, language must reflect the customs and habits of a nation, and idioms are closely related to them. Therefore, English idioms that reflect these customs and habits must have ethnic characteristics. For example, there are many idioms in English related to a nation's sports, entertainment, dietary habits, animals, plants, economy, etc., all of which accurately reflect the ethnic characteristics of idioms. For instance, idioms related to food include "jam tomorrow" (something that is promised but is unlikely to happen), "hard cheese" (unfortunate), "high tea" (an afternoon formal tea), "mother's milk" (good wine, something naturally beloved), "beer and skittles" (fun and entertainment), etc. In English, there are many idioms related to animals, such as "see the elephant" (to see the world), "have bats in the belfry" (to be crazy), "wolf in sheep's clothing" (a malicious person pretending to be kind), "a dead duck" (someone who is doomed), "a little bird told me" (I have heard a secret from someone), "have seen the lions" (to have experienced the world), etc. These idioms reflect this nation's unique concepts and customs.

3.5.3 The Regional Characteristics

Language is both a social and cultural phenomenon. Any culture cannot be separated from its specific natural geographical environment, and will have different characteristics due to its geographical, climatic, and environmental features. English idioms, as the essence of the English language, inevitably reflect distinct regional characteristics.

There are many idioms in English that involve sea, weather, wind, rain, storm, water, such as "in hot water" "any port in a storm" "under the weather" "between the devil and the deep (blue) sea" "as right as rain" "hang in the wind" , and so on. English is an island country with a developed shipping industry. Due to the influence of the warm and humid North Atlantic air current, the UK has abundant precipitation, rain is commonplace, and it is often foggy. Multiple types of weather can occur in a single day, so there are many idioms that reflect this natural environment, all of which have distinct regional characteristics. For example, there is no bamboo in the UK, so it is difficult to associate with it. The Chinese idiom "yǔ hòu chūn sǔn" can only be expressed in English as "to boom like mushrooms" , as a metaphor for things flourishing and developing vigorously.

3.6 Variations of English Idioms

As language constantly evolves with the development of society, idioms, as a part of language, inevitably undergo certain changes, albeit not very noticeable ones. Zhang Peiji (1980) once pointed out that variations of English idioms can be categorized into legitimate and temporary ones. Legitimate variations refer to those that must adhere to the overall meaning and basic structural form of the prototype idiom, and have been accepted by society. For instance, in English, one can say "go bananas" or "drive sb. bananas" to mean "lose control emotionally", and say "to fly in one's own grease" or "to stew in one's juice" to mean "suffer the consequences of one's own actions", and use either "to kick down/away/over the ladder" to mean "betray someone who helped you", or "put oneself in someone else's shoes" to mean "empathize with others". There are other variations of the latter idiom, such as "place (or put) oneself in others' position" or "put oneself in someone else's place." Similarly, "money makes the mare go" can also be expressed as "he who laughs last laughs longest" or "he who laughs last laughs best." These idioms are commonly recognized as legitimate variations.

Apart from legitimate variations, there are temporary ones. Temporary variations refer to changes made to idioms temporarily, to fit a specific context or to achieve a certain rhetorical effect. They are more flexible than legitimate ones, as they can escape the constraints of the overall or basic meaning of the prototype idiom, making language vivid and interesting, and achieving unexpected effects. Omitting or simplifying certain words in an idiom is the most common form of temporary variation. For example, "early birds" in "Early birds roost at the door of the land office in Battleford to ensure the first pick of new tracts" is an abbreviation of the idiom "It's the early bird that catches the worm" (the one who arrives first has the best chance of success), which makes language more concise. Similarly, "the stitch of time" in "Well, it's the old story of the stitch in time" is a simplified version of the idiom "A stitch on time saves nine" (fix a problem early before it becomes worse), which meets the requirements of spoken language. Another form of temporary variation is the replacement of words. It's just another case of "woman proposes, man disposes" is a variation of the idiom "Man proposes, God disposes" (people make plans, but God decides the outcome), in which "man" and "God" are replaced with "woman" and "man," respectively, making language more humorous. Another example, after taking a beating for five rounds, the fighter's seconds threw in the towel. "Throw in the sponge" can also be used instead of "throw in the towel" , and "sponge" can be substituted with "towel."

Additionally, variations can be made by adding words to fit the context, such as in the sentence, "Large police forces were encamped near the meeting, out of sight but hardly out of mind" . The original idiom "out of sight, out of mind" was adapted by adding "but hardly" to break the pattern, to fit the sentence's meaning. This shows how idioms can be flexible in their forms. Other ways to vary idioms include using hyphens, like in the sentence, "John is not a saving boy; he spends his money without thought for the future, and lives a hand-to-mouth life." The original phrase "from hand to mouth" was transformed into an adjective phrase using a hyphen, "hand-to-mouth" .

4 The Rhetorical Study of English Idioms

Idioms are concise, meaningful, and profound expressions, which serve as carriers and reflections of national culture. They are the essence of language, mainly because idioms are a concentrated expression of various rhetorical techniques. Rhetoric originally means modifying speeches, which is a language activity using various language techniques to achieve the best expression effect. It can make language expression more vivid, imaginative, and persuasive. Many rhetorical techniques are used in English idioms, such as rhyme, metaphor, personification, antithesis, hyperbole, metonymy, euphemism, and pun. This chapter mainly explores the rhetorical methods of English idioms from the perspective of rhetorical techniques, namely, from the aspects of phonology and semantics.

4.1 Phonological Rhetoric in English Idioms

Phonological rhetoric are rhetoric techniques created by utilizing the phonetic characteristics of words, mainly including alliteration, assonance, consonance, rhyme, and onomatopoeia. Phonological techniques make language sound rhythmic and catchy, leaving a lasting impression. The following will be analyzed and discussed one by one.

4.1.1 Alliteration

Alliteration, also known as initial rhyme or head rhyme, comes from the Latin phrase *ad literam* (according to the letters), referring to two or more words whose initial letters and pronunciation are the same or similar, producing a pleasant sound. Alliteration only refers to the first part or the first consonant group of the first phoneme being the same. If the first part is completely absent, only the main vowel can be the same. Alliteration is a means of enhancing the rhythm in lines and is a rhythmical auxiliary factor. This is also an important manifestation of the pursuit of form and phonetic beauty in English. In English, the phenomenon of alliteration can appear in noun phrases, verb phrases, adjective phrases, adverb phrases, and proverbs, which are vivid and expressive, easy to pronounce. Alliteration includes the repetition of a single consonant, double consonant repetition, three-sound repetition (same initial consonant+vowel+consonant) and irregular repetition. Some common phrases with alliteration are listed as follows:

first and foremost
safe and sound
tit for tat
neither fish, flesh nor fowl
track and ruin
(with) might and main
saints and sinners
(in) weal and (or) woe
as large as life
as busy as bee
spick and span
bag and baggage
part and parcel

Some common sentences with alliteration are listed as follows:

> No pain, no gain.
> Speech is sliver, silence is gold.
> Time and tide wait for no man.
> Fortune favors the fool.
> wild whirling words
> black and blue
> now and never

4.1.2 End Rhyme

End rhyme, which is equivalent to the Latin word "rhythus", refers to the phenomenon of two or more words with similar pronunciations at the end of words that echo each other due to their position. It is often used to increase the sense of rhythm and achieve the effect of impressing readers with sound. As opposed to alliterations, end rhymes refer to adjacent or closely related words with the ending vowels, consonants, or vowels and consonants being the same. Some English idioms with the same ending vowels and consonants are listed as follows:

> Man proposes, God disposes
> nearest and dearest
> huff and puff
> god disposes

Some English idioms with the same ending vowels are listed as follows:

never ever
high and dry
wear and tear
fair and square

Some English idioms with the same ending consonants are listed as follows:

flotsam and jetsam
out and about

These English idioms with end rhyme are easy and comfortable to read, with a rich musical sense, giving you a sense of beauty and enjoyment.

4.1.3 Assonance

Assonance refers to the rhyme of stressed vowels in two or more words, while the consonants after the vowels are different. There are some such English idioms, such as "quite right" "cut and run", "high time" "Out of sight, out of mind" "Little strokes fell great oaks" "A stitch in time saves nine", and so on. These idioms with assonance can make language rhythmic and appealing.

4.1.4 Consonance

Consonance refers to the rhyme of the same consonants in two or more words, but the vowels before the consonants are different. Examples of idioms with consonance are "odds and ends" "a stroke of luck" "last but not the least" "East or west, home is the best" "Fortune favors fools" "Bread is the staff of life", and so on. These idioms with consonance can give people a relaxed and pleasant feeling, making it easy to remember.

4.1.5 Onomatopoeia

Onomatopoeia refers to words that are formed by imitating the sounds of things or actions. Onomatopoeia can imitate specific or abstract objects. For example, words that imitate sounds people make include "giggle" "murmur" "whimper" and "babble" . Words that imitate the sounds of specific objects include "splash" "rustle" "crack" and "thump" . Words that imitate the sounds of animals include "buzz" "chirp" "mew" "Bowwow" , and so on.

Onomatopoeia makes language concise, lively, and easy to understand. It can give people a real sense of hearing, enhance the strength of language and achieve the effect of conveying emotions through sound.

4.2 Semantic Rhetoric in English Idioms

Semantic rhetoric refers to the rhetorical strategies and techniques that make use of the inherent properties of linguistic units and the semantic relationships between different linguistic units. English idioms are concise, profound, vivid, and rich in meaning mainly because they make use of a large number of semantic rhetorical devices, such as simile, metaphor, personification, antithesis, hyperbole, euphemism, pun, and humor.

4.2.1 Metaphor

Metaphor is a figure of speech that uses concrete, familiar, and easily understood things to explain abstract, complicated, and unfamiliar things by pointing out the similarities between the two. The key to constructing a metaphor is that the two things being compared must be essentially different, but there must be some similarity between them for the metaphor to be valid. A metaphor typically consists of the tenor (the thing being described) and the vehicle (the thing being used to describe it) connected by a comparative word or phrase. Metaphors can be divided into four types: explicit (simile), implicit (metaphor), metonymy, and synecdoche. Metaphor is the most frequently used rhetorical device in English idioms, which makes them more lively, evocative, and easier to understand by turning the plain and complex into the concrete and simple.

4.2.1.1 Simile

Simile compares two different things that have some common feature, and the shared feature exists in the minds of people rather than in the things themselves. A simile typically consists of a comparative word, such as like, as, seem, as if, as though, similar to, such as, the same as, etc., connecting the tenor and the vehicle. For example, "drink like a fish" means drinking an excessive amount of alcohol, in which "drink" is the tenor, "fish" is the vehicle, and "like" is the comparative word. There are many idioms in English that belong to simile, such as "talk like a book" meaning speaking in a formal and academic manner, "as fresh as a rose" meaning full of energy, "smoke like a chimney" meaning smoking heavily, "as proud as a peacock" meaning excessively proud, "as timid as a mouse" meaning very shy, "as clear as crystal" meaning very clear, "as black as pitch" meaning very dark, "as brave as a lion" meaning very brave, "as straight as an arrow" meaning very direct, "feel like a fish out of water" meaning feeling uncomfortable, "sell like hotcakes" meaning very popular and in demand, "as sly as a fox" meaning very cunning, "as faithful as a dog" meaning very loyal, "as slow as a tortoise" meaning very slow, and many others.

By using simile, these idioms express their meanings in a more vivid and concrete way, making a deep impression on people.

4.2.1.2 Metaphor

Metaphor is a comparison between two things by using the name of one thing to refer to another. Its typical form is "A is B", where both the tenor and vehicle appear and there is no explicit comparative word. Common link words include "is" "becomes" "turns into", etc. The essential difference between a metaphor and simile is that the former does not use a comparative word such as "like" or "as", and the comparison is left to the reader to perceive. Metaphors are widely used in English idioms and are a powerful tool for expressing people's thoughts and emotions. Wang Baohua (2001) pointed out that "metaphor is a conceptual tool for people to understand or explain experiences in one domain through experiences in another domain, and it is a tool for people to conceptualize abstract categories". For example, the idiom "castles in the air", without using a comparative word, literally meaning "pavilion in the air" (tenor). It can be imagined that an aerial palace, no matter how much effort is put into its construction, would be very difficult to become a real building. Therefore, this idiom metaphorically refers to "something illusory or imaginary" (vehicle).

Another good example is "cook one's goose". In the eyes of Westerners, goose refers to a foolish and ignorant person, often used as a synonym for "idiot" and "ignorant" and has been frequently used throughout history to mock people's stupidity and uselessness. The idiom has a story behind it. It is said that during the Middle Ages, the King of Sweden led his army to conquer many lands. One day, the army arrived at a certain city, where the defenders decided to hang a goose, symbolizing a "fool", on the high tower of the city wall to ridicule and mock the Swedish King and his army to deflate their confidence. However, this had the opposite effect. The insult fired up the attacking army, who fought even more valiantly and ultimately conquered and destroyed the entire city. And naturally, the hanging goose was cooked in the war's flames. People later used this story to refer to "ruining one's own prospects or sabotaging someone's plans," etc. Through this story, we can learn that in the idiom "cook one's goose", the tenor of is "goose", the vehicle is an event which is "ruining one's own prospects", and no comparative word is used.

"Born with a silver spoon" is a third good example. according to Western customs, rich Europeans used to have a habit of holding a religious ceremony when naming a newborn baby. During the ceremony, they would give the baby a spoon made of silver. The tenor of this idiom is a tangible and concrete object — "a silver spoon", while the vehicle is intangible and abstract — "social status, wealth, etc.", hence the metaphorical meaning of this idiom is "born into wealth and privilege".

There are many English idioms with metaphor employed, such as "a different kettle of fish" "the nineteenth hole" "the pudding house" "above the salt" "high and dry" "to teach to swim" "to plough the sand" "between the devil and the deep sea" "in hot water" "keep your shirt on" "kick the bucket" "let the cat out of the bag" "a wild goose chase" "salt of the earth" "the apple of one's eye" and so on. The greatest feature of these metaphorical idioms is that concrete, vivid, and imagery objects are used to metaphorically describe abstract and complex things, making the language more colloquial and easier to understand and remember.

4.2.1.3 Metonymy

Metonymy is an English figure of speech where, instead of using the name of a thing, a closely related concept is used to represent it. According to Cihai, a Dictionary of Chinese Language, "Metonymy is one of the rhetorical figures, where a thing A is not similar to a thing B, but they have an inseparable relationship. By using this relationship, the name of thing B is used to represent thing A." The typical form of metonymy is to substitute the tenor with the vehicle, without mentioning the tenor directly. Metonymy emphasizes the characteristics of the thing itself or its special relationship with other things. Metonymy can be classified into the following four types:

a. Body parts represents their related functions

There are many English idioms in which different parts of the body are used to represent a person or thing, such as head, eyes, hands, ears, nose, shoulders, legs, etc. For example, "Pay through the nose" literally means "to pay with one's nose", which implies a great cost or expense. It also means "to pay a large amount" or "to pay a high price". Similarly, "pay/cost an arm and a leg" also implies a substantial expense, as if one were sacrificing a body part. Despite the lack of direct connection between the nose, arms, and legs and the act of spending money, these expressions utilize body parts figuratively to convey the idea of something being expensive. "Bite the hand that feeds you" refers to the ungracious act of returning someone's kindness with harm or ingratitude. The "hand" in this expression typically refers to someone who has provided help or support.

Other similar examples include "break a leg" (good luck), "shoe is on the other foot" (the situation has changed), "stick your neck out" (to take a risk or ask for criticism), "get cold feet" (to become scared or timid), "be armed to the teeth" (to be fully equipped with weapons), "head and shoulders above someone" (to be better than someone), "be all ears" (to listen attentively), "bite your tongue" (to refrain from speaking), "all thumbs" (clumsy), "two-faced" (hypocritical), "splitting hairs" (being overly precise), "put your money where your mouth is" (to back up your words with action), and so on.

  b. Someone's name refers to a certain category

  For example, "Johnny-on-the-spot" literally means "John who is always present" and its metaphoric meaning is a quick-thinking person. The "Johnny" does not refer to a specific person, but is instead used as a metaphor for a "good assistant" . "Keep up with the Joneses" refers to people with similar social status and economic conditions as oneself, typically meaning common people, but with a strong sense of "keeping up with one's neighbors". "Have the Midas touch" refers to the ability or luck to make money, named after King Midas in Greek mythology who was given a power that turned everything he touched into gold. This phrase is used to metaphorically describe someone who can turn anything they touch into gold. "Tom, Dick and Harry" are generic names used to refer to any person. Other English idioms of this kind include "Jack someone around" (to deceive someone), "Lazy Susan" (a revolving circular tray used for serving food on a table), "a plain Jane" (an ordinary-looking woman), "a doubting Thomas" (a skeptical person), "All shall be well; Jack shall have Jill" (a saying meaning that all will be well and lovers will be reunited), "Every Jack has his Jill" (a saying indicating that there is a perfect match for everyone), "Jack of all trades, and master of none" (someone who tries to do everything but is not an expert in any particular field), "Jack and Jill" (a boy and girl), and so on.

c. Place names refer to local products or events that have taken place there

For example, "meet one's Waterloo" refers to a complete failure, and Waterloo is the place where the English, Austrian, Prussian, French, and Russian armies allied to defeat Napoleon near the town of Waterloo. Napoleon lost everything as a result and eventually died due to illness. Therefore, Waterloo is used as a metaphor for the failure of war. Other examples include "It's all Greek to me" (it's incomprehensible), "go Dutch" (each paying for oneself), "Chinese Whispers" (rumors and gossip with no basis in fact), "talk for England" (someone who is very talkative and persuasive), "Dutch Courage" (drinking to boost one's courage), "slow boat to China" (taking a very long time to accomplish something), and so on.

d. Location names refer to governments, organizations, or companies.

For example, the Kremlin refers to the Russian government, Fleet Street refers to the British news media, and Hollywood refers to the American film industry.

4.2.1.4 Synecdoche

According to the definition in the Oxford Dictionary, synecdoche is a rhetorical device where a part is used to represent the whole, or the whole is used to represent a part, a single item is used to represent a category, and a material is used to represent the product made from it. Synecdoche is a figure of speech where a word or phrase is substituted with another that is closely related, such as using a part to represent the whole, e.g. "earn one's bread" where bread is a part of essential living, used to represent all food; "Two heads are better than one" where "heads" is used to represent "intellect" ; "Four eyes see more than two" where "eyes" is used to represent "people" ; "Cat's paw" where "paw" represents those who are exploited by others; "a green hand" where "hand" is used to represent "a person" ; "Great minds think alike" where "minds" is used to represent "people" ; "Many hands make light work" where "hand" is used to represent "people" . Using a category to represent another category, such as "poor creature" where "creature" is used to represent "person" ; "Kill two birds with one stone" where "bird" represents "the goal" and "stone" represents "the means, tool or method" . Using a material to represent the product made from it, such as "Do you have any coppers?" where "copper" represents "the coins or small change made from copper" ; "a foe worthy of sb.'s steel" where "steel" is used to represent "sword" .

4.2.2 Analogy

The rhetoric of analogy involves comparing humans to objects, objects to humans, or transforming one object into another. This technique adds unique flavor and makes the described subjects vivid and lifelike. Metaphors are divided into two kinds: personification and objectification.

4.2.2.1 Personification

Personification refers to writing about objects as if they were people, giving them human speech, actions, thoughts, and emotions. Using words that are typically used to describe people can give concrete things a personality, make the language more vivid and imaginative, and make what is being expressed come to life, leaving a strong impression on readers and eliciting an echo in readers' feelings. In English idioms, it is common that words that describe people are used to describe objects. For example, in the idiom "Failure is the mother of success", "Mother" is used to describe the relationship between failure and success, making abstract concepts more concrete and easier to understand. In the idiom "Actions speak louder than words", "Actions" refers to "actions" themselves, which are lifeless and cannot speak. Here, they are personified, giving them human characteristics, making the language more lively and interesting.

Other examples of this type of idiom include "Time is the father of truth", "The pot calls the kettle black", "Where might is master, justice is servant", "Fortune favors fools", "The afternoon knows what the morning never suspected", and "Money makes the mare go". "Truth is the daughter of time".

4.2.2.2 Objectification

Objectification refers to the practice of describing a person as if they were an object or describing object A as if it were object B. This can make language more vivid and give it an animated quality. For example, "break one's word", "eat one's words", "breathe a word", and so on.

4.2.3 Hyperbole

In the *Oxford Advanced English-Chinese Dictionary*, hyperbole is defined as "exaggerated statement that is made for special effect and is not meant to be taken literally". Intentionally exaggerating or minimizing the nature, characteristics, etc. of an existing thing is beneficial for revealing the essence of things, setting the atmosphere, and vividly expressing the author's emotional attitude towards things, increasing the liveliness of language. Some English idioms in which hyperbole is used are as follows: "a single slip brings eternal regret", where "eternal" is an exaggerated usage meaning "forever, everlasting" ; "have one's heart in one's boots" literally meaning "heart beating inside boots", which is logically impossible and therefore a form of exaggeration, used to express someone's extreme nervousness to the point where their heart feels like it's in their boots. The meaning has extended to "extremely nervous" ; "Rain cats and dogs" literally means cats and dogs falling out of the air. We can imagine that it rains as if cats and dogs are falling out of the air, and it must be a lot of rain as if "downpour" in an exaggerate expression, and "rain cats and dogs" metaphorically means it's raining heavily, which is another example of hyperbole used to highlight the feature of something and trigger endless imagination. Other examples are listed as follows: "cry one's eyes out" "bring the house down" "a flood of tears" "have a sea of trouble" "It was sick of my soul" "be scared to death" "make a mountain out of a molehill" "beat one's brains out" "go through the roof" "A stitch in time saves nine" "Every lover sees a thousand graces in the beloved" "The woman can kill three men with simply two words" "A drop of ink may make a million think" , and so on.

4.2.4 Parallelism

Parallelism refers to three or more elements forming a parallel structure in a sentence or clause, with no strict word count but rather a focus on combining similar and related clauses or elements. This technique can enhance language and strengthen expression, with English proverbs such as "Tell me, and I'll forget. show me, and I may not remember. involve me, and I'll understand" "Kind hearts are the garden; kind thoughts are the roots; kind words are the flowers; kind deeds are the fruits" "Make all you can, save all you can, give all you can" and "Wash a dog, comb a dog, still a dog, remains a dog" .

4.2.5 Antithesis

Antithesis refers to two phrases or sentences that have the same or similar structure and related or opposite meanings are arranged symmetrically together. They have a clear rhythm, are expressive, and have harmonious sound, making them easy to recite and remember. English idioms in which the rhetorical device of parallelism is used include "neither fish nor fowl" "from top to toe" "much cry and little wool" "ups and downs" "through thick and thin" "now or never" "far and near" "fast and loose" "rob Peter to pay Paul" and "all brawn and no brains" , and so on. English proverbs in which parallelism is used include "once bitten, twice shy" "where liberty is, there is my country" "two's company, three's crowd" "no root, no fruit" "where there is a will, there is a way" "soon learnt, soon forgotten" "out of debt, out of danger" and "easy come, easy go" .

4.2.6 Repetition

Repetition of a word or sentence is used to emphasize a certain meaning or feeling. There are two types of repetitions: continuous and intermittent. In continuous repetition, there are no other words between the repeated word or sentence, such as "go-go" "so-so" "talkee-talkee" and "goody-goody." In intermittent repetition, there are other words between the repeated word or sentence, such as "again and again" "end to end" "diamond cut diamond" "thus and thus" "neck and neck" "call a spade a spade" "through and through" , and so on.

4.2.7 Irony

Irony means is the use of words or phrases that express a meaning opposite to the intended meaning in order to emphasize the message in a contradictory way. It can be used to satirize, reveal truth, or express friendly intimacy. Irony can come in the forms of semantic irony, situational irony, or dramatic irony.

Semantic irony is the use of words that have an opposite meaning to convey a different meaning. For example, in his book Oliver Twist, Charles Dickens ironically used the rhetoric of irony in his statement, "What a noble illustration of the tender laws of his favoured country! — they let the paupers go to sleep". Here, the author used terms such as noble, tender, and favoured in an opposite way to satirize British law of the time, indicating that poor people had only the right to be unemployed and sleep, contrasting with the previous gentle and considerate tone and expressing Charles Dickens' dissatisfaction with society in a mocking way.

Situational irony mainly derives from the speaker's attitude in a specific situation. For example, during a date, a man asked a woman why she liked him, and the woman said, "You are such a bad man (boy)." In this situation, the woman's statement is not meant to convey that the man is actually bad, but rather it is a case of saying the opposite of what is meant, expressing intimacy and friendliness through teasing.

Dramatic irony refers to the words spoken by a character in a book or drama that are true in and of themselves, but due to the reader or audience knowing more about the situation, they realize that what the character is saying is the opposite of the reality, and this serves to create a humorous or sad effect. For instance, in Mark Twain's famous book, The Adventures of Tom Sawyer, there is a conversation between Tom's friend Sid and his Aunt Polly where Sid says, "I hope Tom is better off where he is, but if he'd been better in some way." "Sid!" Tom felt the glare of the old lady's eye, though he could not see it. "Not a word against my Tom, now that he's gone!" Here, Sid's statement is the truth as far as he knows, since he thinks that Tom has died. His conversation partner, Aunt Polly, also thinks the same. However, readers know the opposite is true because Tom is actually hiding under the bed.

4.2.8 Euphemism

The word Euphemism originated from Greece. The morpheme "eu" means good, while "pheme" refers to speech. "euphemism" means "good speech" or "comfortable words" . *The Oxford Concise Dictionary* (1976) defines it as follows: "Substitution of mild or vague or roundabout expression for harsh or direct one; expression thus substituted" , which means the use of milder and more gentle words to replace some blunt or harsh words.

It is commonly used in everyday life's taboo language, polite language, and politics, such as diseases, aging, death, human excretory reproductive organs, social occupations, crimes, and economic, political, and military aspects. There are many euphemisms in English idioms, such as "die," which is a word that people avoid. When people hear this word, they are unhappy. In English-speaking countries, there are many idioms, such as "close one's day, pay the debt of nature, depart to God, go to a better world, go to sleep, pass away" which are euphemistic expressions of "death" . Euphemistic expressions for going to the toilet (urinating and defecating) include "wash one's hands, relieve oneself, get some fresh air, answer the call of nature, make water, pass water, see the moon, make a coke stop, bathroom, washroom, restroom, his and hers, go to necessary house, WC, go to spend a penny". Polite expressions for pregnancy include "She is expecting, She is in a family way, She is in an interesting/delicate condition, She has canceled all her social engagements, She has had an accident (for unmarried women)". Polite expressions for the elderly include "elderly, senior, seasoned, and old age pensioner". Instead of saying "ugly", we use "plain, homely, not particularly good-looking". Instead of saying "fat", we say "plump, chubby, stout, or heavyset". Expressions for "poverty" include "low in one's pocket" and "in an awkward financial situation", while expressions for "not having money" include "hard for money" and "pinched for money". There are many other related euphemisms, such as "cross the Jordan, look off-color" (unwell), "social disease" (AIDS), "domestic engineer" (homemaker), "displaced person" (refugee), "land architect" (gardener), "pass air/let a breeze/make noise" (flatulence), "superintendent/custodian" (janitor), "a slow learner/underachiever" (poor student), "exceptional/special child" (mentally challenged child), and so on.

4.2.9 Pun

In the *Longman Dictionary of Contemporary English*, pun is defined as "An amusing use of a word or phrase that has two meanings, or of words with the same sound but different meanings". Puns are a common rhetorical device in English that use homonyms, homophones, polysemy, and ambiguity to achieve the goal of a "double meaning". Semantic puns can be used in stories, poetry, riddles, jokes, advertisements, and nursery rhymes as well as in formal occasions. It is a rhetorical device that people around the world love, as it can make language witty, funny, vivid, and humorous, while also expressing serious thoughts and profound emotions. There are mainly three types of puns.

4.2.9.1 Homophonic Puns

Homophonic pun refers to the use of two words with the same sound but different meanings in the same context to create a pun. For example:

a. On Sunday they pray for you and on Monday they prey on you.

The pronunciation of pray is the same as that of prey, while they have different meanings, with pray meaning address a solemn request, and prey meaning exploitation. By using the homophones "pray" and "prey" , the sentence can achieve the effect of satirizing the hypocritical face of gentlemen and ladies in Western churches.

b. A: What starts with T, ends with T, and is full of T?

B: Teapot.

The last letter "T" here sounds the same as the word "tea" , belonging to homophones with different meanings and spellings, which is a homophonic pun.

c. A bicycle can't stand on its own because it's two-tyred.

"Two-tyred" and "too tired" form a homophonic word, so this sentence can be understood as "This bicycle ridden by its owner for a long time can't stand on its own because it's too tired". The use of homophonic puns with different meanings and spellings in this sentence achieves a humorous effect.

4.2.9.2 Homographic Puns

Homographic puns refer to the humorous puns formed by using two meanings of the same word in the same context. For example:

d. A: What is the difference between a soldier and a young girl?

B: One powders the face, the other faces the powders.

Powder can be both a noun and a verb. In this sentence, as a verb, "powder" means "to apply powder" , and as a noun, it means a kind of substance called "powder" . The word plays on both meanings of the word to create humor.

e. A: Why is a river rich?

B: Because it has two banks.

"Bank" is a homograph with the same sound and shape but different meanings, referring to both "a financial institution" and "the sloping land alongside a river", which creates a humorous effect.

4.2.9.3 Double Entendre

Double entendre refers to intentionally or unintentionally using the phenomenon of words having multiple meanings to misinterpret the intentions of the person speaking, resulting in subtle ambiguity in the context, in order to achieve humorous or sarcastic effects.

For example, when a professor tapped on his desk and shouted, "Gentlemen, order!", the entire class yelled "Beer!" Here, the students intentionally misinterpreted the professor's intentions. The professor's actual intention was to ask the students to be quiet, but by using the language similar to that used in a bar when customers place an order, the students intentionally misinterpreted it as the other meaning and responded with "Beer". The students answered in a way that did not directly address the professor's words, skillfully resolving the awkward situation at the time.

When someone asks, "Can you see a female?" and the other person responds, "Of course, I can see a female as easily as a male. Do you suppose I'm blind?" Here, the second person uses a double entendre with the word "see" to misinterpret the intention of the first person. In the first sentence, "see" means to have an appointment with, while the second person understands "see" in the sense of "being able to see". This answer may inevitably make the first person feel embarrassed.

In short, the reasons why English idioms are vivid, persuasive and expressive is mainly due to the use of various rhetorical techniques.

5 Pragmatic Analysis of English Idioms

English idioms often appear in the form of word blocks, which are conventional, and they reflect the unique cultural characteristics of English-speaking countries. Moreover, English idioms possess rich pragmatic values and implications. In the process of interpersonal communication, the correct use of English idioms can make language more concise, humorous, and vivid. However, mastering and flexibly applying English idioms is not an easy task because these idioms have their own uniqueness, which is mainly reflected in semantic specificity, cultural connotations, diverse types, and widespread application. Pragmatics is the study of language use in context. It is a new discipline. John Langshaw Austin, a British philosopher, officially proposed the concept of the theory of pragmatics in 1955. Since then, many scholars have paid attention to it and have put forward a series of new theories such as implicature, cooperative principle, politeness principle, speech act theory, relevance theory, adaptation theory, meme theory, etc. This chapter will analyze English idioms from the perspective of pragmatics, namely speech act theory, conversational implicature theory, and relevance theory.

5.1 Speech Act Theory and English Idioms

The Speech Act theory was first proposed by the English philosopher Austin in the 50s of the 20th century, which was inherited, perfected and developed by his student, the American philosopher John

Searle, who discussed the relationship between words and deeds, speech and action. Austin argued that when a person spoke, the person actually completed three behaviors, namely the locutionary act, the illocutionary act and the perlocutionary act. The locutionary act of speech refers to the meaning of the sentence itself. The illocutionary act refers to the intention of saying the sentence, that is, the implicit meaning conveyed by the sentence. The perlocutionary act refers to the effect achieved by saying the sentence. Among these three behaviors, Austin was most concerned with perlocutionary speech acts, which he considered to be the most important. He classified perlocutionary speech acts into five categories based on the illocutionary force of the utterance: verdictives, executives, commissives, behabitives, and expositives. Searle, however, believed that Austin's categorization was somewhat ambiguous, and further classified speech acts into five categories: representatives, commissives, directives, declarations, and expressives. Representatives express the speaker's judgments, statements of fact, or conclusions, and enable the speaker to adapt their speech to the external world and express their perception and views of the surrounding world. Commissives refer to the speaker's commitment to do something and enable the external world to adapt to the speaker's speech, such as commitments, threats, and oaths. Directives are the speaker's attempt to get the listener to do something and enable the external world to adapt to the listener's speech, such as commands, requests, and suggestions. Declarations are intended to change the current state of the entity mentioned and enable the speaker's speech to change the external world, such as naming, blessing, and marriage. Expressives express the speaker's psychological state or attitude towards the situation involved, enabling the speaker's speech to adapt to their psychological world, such as greetings, congratulations, thanks and apologies.

English idioms are fixed phrases or short sentences refined by language after a long period of use, with profound meaning, the essence of national culture, and the crystallization of the collective wisdom of the people. At the same time, many English idioms have become idiomatic expressions in our daily communication, which are used to express commands, suggestions, advice, warnings, requests, notices, thanks, threats, politeness, wishes, curses and other verbal acts. The following describes the situation of English idioms to express verbal behavior.

5.1.1 Representatives

Representatives mainly refers to statements or descriptions of situations that the speaker believes to be true, such as assertions, statements, and descriptions. Proverbs and aphorisms in English idioms belong to the category of representive speech acts. For example:

1) The supreme happiness of life is the conviction that we are loved.

2) Nearly all men can stand adversity, but if you want to test a man's character, give him power.

3) Easier said than done.

4) Where there is a will, there is a way.

5) One false step will make a great difference.

6) Slow and steady wins the race.

7) A fall into the pit, a gain in your wit.

8) Life is the art of drawing sufficient conclusions form insufficient premises.

9) The good or ill of man lies within his own will.

10) The proper function of man is to live, not to exist.

5.1.2 Commissives

Commissives mainly refers to the behavior where the speaker promises certain actions in the future, such as making a vow, issuing a threat, or making a commitment. There are many such expressions in English, such as "I promise..." "If you are..., I would..." "I would..." "How comes it that..." "How dare you..." "What do you mean by..." , etc. These are common idioms used to implement verbal behaviors such as making a vow, issuing a threat, and making a commitment. Some examples of English idioms used to express commissives are:

1) Leave me alone, if you know what is good for you.

2) If you dare go on gambling with those guys, I will beat you black and blue.

3) Promise that you will never be late again or I will fire you.

4) How dare you talk to me like that?

5) How comes it that you always taking away my things without asking?

6) What do you mean by messing up all the things on my desk?

7) Make my day.

8) If you value your life, never say one word.

5.1.3 Directives

Directives mainly refers to trying to make the listener do something, such as making requests, invitations, commands, suggestions, advice, prohibitions, orders, etc. There are many such expressions in English, such as "You ought to..." "You could/should..." "I recommend you to..." "You'd better do something" "I suggest/advise you to do something" "Why not..." , etc. Some examples of English idioms used to express directives are:

1) You mustn't do that!
2) Don't do that!
3) If I were you, I would...
4) Do you think it might be a good idea to...?
5) Have you tried doing it this way?
6) Would you mind if I say something...?
7) Do it or else.
8) Come and have... with us.
9) How about giving me a nice kiss?
10) Why no come and see me tomorrow?

5.1.4 Declarations

Declarations mainly refers to sudden changes caused by speaking, such as appointment, dismissal, announcement, nomination, naming, etc. The verbs in English that express declarative speech acts include name, declare, pronounce, dismiss, nominate, appoint, resign, and so on.

Some examples of English idioms used to express declarations are:

1) I declare the meeting open.
2) I fire you.

3) I name this ship Elizabeth.

4) I sentence you to five-year hard labor.

5) I declare war on your country.

5.1.5 Expressives

Expressives mainly refer to expressing emotions and attitudes towards a certain situation, such as thanking, congratulating, greeting, apologizing, wishing, feeling joy, surprise, anger and other verbal behaviors... Some examples of English idioms used to express expressives are:

1) Have a good time!

2) Give my beat wishes to you.

3) How is everything going?

4) God bless you!

5) Cheer up!

6) Oh, my God.

7) Excuse me.

8) Thank you very much!

9) I am thankful to you for your kindness.

10) I greatly appreciate your timely help.

11) It's very kind of you to come and help us.

12) I really don't think we could manage it without your help.

13) Please accept our thank for...

14) May every special happiness fill this day for you and may the year bring everything you look forward to.

15) You did/made it!

16) Well done!

17) May I make my sincere congratulation on your excellent achievement?

18) Keep your fingers crossed.

19) Break a leg.

20) How is everything (with you)?

21) How are you feeling?

22) What's up?

23) What is going on these days?

24) I think it is about time for us to go now.

25) I really enjoy the meal.

26) Thank you for everything.

27) I am glad to meet you here.

In addition, another important aspect of Speech Act Theory is the theory of Indirect Speech Act, proposed by Searle. Searle (1979) stated that an action that is indirectly performed by implementing another action is called an Indirect Speech Act. Indirect Speech Acts include Literal Force and Illocutionary Force, and in order to understand Indirect Speech Acts, one must first understand the Literal Force of a sentence and then derive the Illocutionary Force from it. Some Indirect Speech Acts have a great deal of conventionality, and the Illocutionary Force can be directly derived from the Literal Force of the sentence by its syntactical form and habitual use. This is called Conventional Indirect Speech Act. In contrast, there are also Non-Conventional Indirect Speech Acts, which mainly rely on the context or common knowledge between the speakers to derive their Indirect Illocutionary Force.

There are many English idioms and expressions that are essential for daily communication with their various forms, rich content, and high frequency of use. People dislike being commanded to do something directly, so when requesting or commanding someone to do something, they generally use a more indirect way of expression, such as saying "Can you pass me the salt?" rather than "Pass me the salt." This indirect way of expression is more pleasant for others to hear, and they are naturally more willing to help. For instance, saying "No" directly to refuse a friend's request may seem impolite, whereas saying "I'm afraid I can't" achieves the same effect of refusal without offending anybody. There are many idioms in English that use Indirect Speech Acts to convey their meaning, such as:

1) Can you hold, please?
2) I couldn't be more sure.
3) Don't play games with me!
4) We'd better be off.
5) Don't take it to heart.
6) After you.
7) I'm not going to kid you.
8) No ifs, ands or buts.
9) When did your last servant die?
10) Has the cat got your tongue?

In addition, there are some proverbs and colloquialisms in which indirect verbal acts are used to express the speaker's intention. For example,

1) A beautiful thing is never perfect.

2) A lazy youth, a lousy age.

3) A little neglect may bread great mischief.

4) A man is not good or bad for one action.

5) Life is not all roses. Life is not a good road.

6) Penny wise, pound foolish.

7) Put not your hand between the bark and the tree.

8) To think of danger in time of peace.

9) What you don't see with your eyes, don't invent with your mouth.

10) Work today, for you know not how much you may be hindered tomorrow.

English idioms are often used in everyday communication because they convey not only illocutionary acts, such as representatives, commissives, directives, declarations, and expressives, but also indirect verbal behaviors. The correct and appropriate use of English idioms allows people to communicate efficiently and smoothly. The examples provided above illustrate that speech act theory are used to express the speaker's intended meaning in many idioms, proverbs, and colloquialisms in English.

5.2 Conversational Implicature Theory and English Idioms

5.2.1 Introduction

In 1957, American philosopher of language Grice proposed in his article "Meaning" that meaning could be divided into natural meaning and non-natural meaning. Non-natural meaning consists of both literal meaning and implied meaning. In pragmatics, people focus on the non-natural meaning of discourse in speech communication. Levinson (1983, p.131) pointed out that non-natural meaning includes literal meaning and implicature meaning. Meaning can be divided into conventional meaning and non-conventional meaning. Conventional meaning is determined by the customary meaning of words and is close to the "explicit meaning", while non-conventional meaning includes non-conversational meaning and conversational meaning. Conversational meaning is divided into general conversational meaning and specific conversational meaning. General conversational meaning refers to conversational meaning that can be generated without special context or relevant background knowledge, while specific conversational meaning refers to conversational meaning that requires context or relevant background knowledge to be generated.

In 1975, Grice proposed the cooperative principle. Grice believed that in the process of communication, people need to have an understanding in complete harmony, a principle they both follow to ensure the smooth progress of discourse and successful communication, which is the cooperative principle. The cooperative principle includes the following: the maxim of quantity providing sufficient information needed for communication; the maxim of quality which means not saying something one believes to be false or lacking evidence; the maxim of relevance which means saying something that is relevant; and the maxim of manner avoiding vagueness, ambiguity, and expressing oneself clearly, concisely, and orderly.

However, in actual communication, it's impossible for both parties to always follow the cooperative principle when speaking. Later, Grice proposed the theory of conversational implicature. The generation of conversational meaning is due to the fact that people do not strictly adhere to the cooperative principle and its related rules for various reasons during real communication. When a speaker intentionally violates the cooperative principle, the listener needs to understand the speaker's implicatures to continue the conversation normally. The theory of conversational implicature focuses on the speaker's communicative intentions and the true meaning of the discourse understood by the listener. It is the core content of pragmatic research. To comprehensively and deeply study the meaning of speech in communication, it's necessary to study both the literal and implied meaning of speech, with the implied meaning taking on the greatest significance. Conversational implicature has the following characteristics: cancellability, which means a conversational implicature can be canceled by adding a clause or the speaker indicating abandoning it through context; non-detachability, which means conversational implicature attaches to the content of speech, not the form of speech, so it's impossible to change the implicature by changing the form of speech revealing the same content; calculability, which means the listener can deduce the corresponding conversational implicature based on the literal meaning of speech and the various principles of the cooperative principle; indeterminacy, which means that conversational implicature change according to different contexts; and non-conventionality, which means that conversational implicatures are not literal meaning nor a part of the literal meaning. Instead, they are derived through combining the principles of the cooperative principle, the literal meaning of speech, and the context.

5.2.2 Analysis of English Idioms According to the Conversational Implicature Theory

It is sometimes impossible to understand the meaning of English idioms literally, because English idioms themselves are characterized with semantic specificity and cultural inheritance. English idioms will be further analyzed through conversational implicature theory, revealing some characteristics of English idioms. For example,

1) A: I want to change my job. My salary is too low.

B: You should wait until you know the ropes.

In the conversation, A said he wants to change jobs because the salary is too low. B responded, "You need to wait until you know the ropes." If A doesn't understand this phrase and takes it literally, he won't be able to fully understand what B means. The original meaning of "rope" is a cord, which is extended to mean "essentials" or "rules" in this context. Therefore, "know the ropes" means to be experienced and skillful in a particular field.

2) A: Hey, look at my new invention. It may be the biggest watch in the world.

B: But where's the beef?

In the conversation, A says, "Look at my new invention. It may be the biggest watch in the world" . B's response "But where's the beef?" is meant to convey "But where is its real value?" instead of its literal meaning. Both of Bs' responses in example (1) and (2) seem to violate the relevant principles of cooperative communication, as they appear unrelated to what A said. However, in face, Bs are using an English idiom to respond to As, and only As' comprehension of these idioms can keep the conversation going smoothly.

3) A: How is your football game going today?

B: Quite bad. I was always losing my edge in the game.

A: Take it easy. Maybe you are just too tired these days.

"lose my edge" said by B does not mean "no blade" , but "not in good shape, not at a normal level" .

4) A: How can Jack be employed by that big company? He didn't even go to college.

B: His boss was impressed with his rich horse sense.

In the conversation, B uses the English idiom "horse sense", which is equivalent to common sense, signifying "common sense, the experience of daily life." This idiom originates from the curious idea that people used to think that horses have low intelligence, so anything that even a horse could recognize or judge would certainly be common sense.

In the two conversations above, although B does not violate some of the norms in the principle of cooperation, only in the context can A understand what B is trying to express.

5) hit it off

The idiom *hit it off* is used to indicate the similarity of temperament between people, and can be used to describe a variety of interpersonal relationships, which can describe both friendship and love. For example,

She is a kind girl, so she **hits it off** well with everybody. (She's a kind girl, so she gets along well with everyone.)

6) Put on the dog

This idiom comes from the American Civil War, when a large number of nouveau riche liked to spend a lot of money on a rare breed of puppy to show their financial power. Some wealthy ladies often hold a small dog on their laps to show off their affluence when receiving guests. At that time, students at Yale University created the phrase "to put on the dog" to mock those newly rich individuals, making fun of those high-society women who couldn't wait to show off their precious dogs as if they were pieces of clothing. The literal meaning of "put on the dog" is to "wear a dog", which implies showing off for others, and it's extended to mean "putting on airs" or "showing off wealth". For example, I had this friend in the army who was the son of one of the richest men in the country. But what I like about him was that he never put on the dog to show off his money.

7) to put your money where your mouth is

This idiom originated in the United States during the 1930s. It is a less formal way to tell others not to talk big. If one wants to prove that their words are true, it would be better to prove it with money, provide evidence, or take actual actions. This is an example including this idiomatic expression: The governor of our State talks about the need to improve public education but puts no money where his mouth is. He simply uses education as a reason to raise taxes but he never intends to spend money on it.

8) sock away (deposit in case you need it).

The phrase *sock away* may come from a bygone era when banks were less common. At that time, some people would hide their savings in an old sock and press it under the mattress for emergency use. Hence the phrase "sock away" was generated to broadly refer to saving a bit of money for other purposes. Of course, modern people rarely keep their savings in socks; most people would deposit it in a bank. For example,

I don't make a lot of money but every week when I get paid I try to sock away ten dollars in my savings account at the bank to buy a ring for the girl I want to marry.

9) raincheck

The idiomatic use of "Raincheck" originates from American baseball games. If it starts raining halfway through a baseball game, players and fans alike have to scramble to find a place to shelter from the rain. If the rain continues incessantly, the game has to be cancelled. As fans leave the stadium, they receive a special ticket called a "raincheck" . With this raincheck, they can re-enter to watch a game for free another time. Although "raincheck" comes from baseball, it has gradually been widely applied in other areas, such as business and social life. For example,

I' d love to go out with you, Ben. I' m sorry, I' m busy tonight but I hope you' ll give me a raincheck.

10) snow job

In British slang, job, in addition to the proper meaning of "work, occupation" , also denotes "illicit (secret or deceptive) actions, criminal behaviors." "Snow" is another slang term, signifying "to confuse or deceive someone with sweet talk, especially flattering words." Here, "snow job" means "deceiving or persuading others through flattery, exaggeration, and other tactics." This phrase can be used not only to sell goods or swindle money, but also to curry favor with bosses or win over women who are easily swayed. Therefore, it is common in daily life. For example,

The swindler did a snow job on the inexperienced shop assistant and sold all his fakes to her.

5.2.3 English Idioms and the Polite Principle

Grice proposed the cooperative principle and the theory of conversational implicature, but he did not explain why people violate the conversational maxims, expressing themselves in an indirect and implicit manner. To this end, Leech proposed the Politeness Principle in 1983. The Politeness Principle has its own maxims and sub-maxims, as follows:

a. Tact Maxim: Minimize the expression of views that are detrimental to others. The sub-maxims are: Try to minimize harm to others; try to maximize benefit to others.

b. Generosity Maxim: Minimize the expression of self-serving views. The sub-maxims are: Try to minimize benefits to oneself; try to maximize harm to oneself.

c. Approbation Maxim: Minimize the expression of disapproval of others. The sub-maxims are: Try to minimize criticism of others; try to maximize praise of others.

d. Modesty Maxim: Minimize praise of oneself. The sub-maxims are: Try to minimize praise of oneself; try to maximize self-deprecation.

e. Agreement Maxim: Minimize disagreement with others. The sub-maxims are: Try to minimize disagreement; try to maximize agreement.

f. Sympathy Maxim: Minimize antipathy between oneself and others. The sub-maxims are: Try to minimize annoyance to the other; try to maximize sympathy for the other. The sub-maxims are: Try to minimize annoyance to the other; try to maximize sympathy for the other.

There are many idiomatic expressions in English that express the meaning of "politeness" , such as idiomatic expressions for wishing, greeting, congratulating, and other daily communication. These idiomatic expressions have become part of English idioms and are frequently used in daily conversations. The embodiment of English idioms in the Politeness Principle is as follows:

a. The embodiment of "Tact, Generosity, Modesty Maxims" in communication through idioms.

In communication, people need to try to minimize harm to others, maximize benefits to others; or try to minimize praise of oneself, maximize self-deprecation; or try to minimize benefits to oneself, maximize harm to oneself. The idioms in the following examples achieve the pragmatic effects of "tact, generosity, modesty" . For example:

1) Could you give me a sheet of paper?
2) Can I help you?
3) Would you like to order now?
4) Could I have the bill, please?
5) Could you tell me...?
6) May I see your passport, please?
7) How stupid of me!
8) May I just have a look?
9) I'm afraid I can't.
10) Could you give me five minutes?
11) Would you mind opening the window?
12) Can you hold, please?
13) Would you like to sit beside me?
14) I wonder if you could do me a favor

b. The embodiment of "Agreement and Approbation Principles" in idioms during communication

In communication, people should try to belittle others less and praise others as much as possible; or try to reduce the disagreement between the two parties as much as possible and increase their agreement. The idioms in the following sentences play a "consensus, praise" pragmatic effect. For example:

1) Thank you very much.
2) Thank you for your kindness.
3) Thank you for being so understanding.
4) Well done!
5) I don't know how I can thank you enough.
6) I do appreciate your help.
7) It's very kind of you.
8) It's my pleasure. / With pleasure. / My pleasure.
9) I do appreciate your precious time.
10) I'm at your service.
11) Thank you for your praise.
12) Congratulations on your engagement.
13) Hearty congratulation on your...
14) I was very pleased to hear...
15) It is good news that...
16) You are right.
17) I agree with you.
18) What a marvelous meal you cooked.
19) You could be a bit more careful.

c. The embodiment of the "Sympathy Principle" in idioms during communication

In communication, people should try to minimize their annoyance towards the other party and maximize their sympathy for them. The idioms in the following sentences play a "sympathy" pragmatic effect. For example:

1) I'm awfully sorry to hear your bad news.
2) I'm sorry about this.
3) I am sorry.
4) I am very sorry to have caused you so much trouble.
5) Sorry to interrupt you. / Sorry to disturb you.
6) Sorry to have kept you waiting.
7) I was deeply sorry to hear...
8) I was deeply grieved to hear...
9) Sending you a special message of sympathy.
10) With sincere sympathy.
11) Please accept my deepest sympathy.
12) Extending deepest sympathy.

5.3 Relevance Theory and English Idioms

Dan Sperber of the University of Paris and Deirdre Wilson of the University of London formally proposed the Relevance Theory in "Relevance: Communication and Cognition" in 1986. They proposed the ostensive-inferential communication model, which replaced the traditional code model. The ostensive-inferential communication model posits that a complete communication process should be a process of "ostension" and "inference". For the speaker, communication is an ostensive act, in which the speaker indicates his or her communicative intention. For the listener, communication is a process of inference, in which the listener deduces the speaker's communicative intention based on the information provided by the speaker. Sperber and Wilson also defined relevance from three perspectives: context, communicative individuals, and phenomena.

The Relevance Theory holds that the relevance of discourse depends on contextual effects and processing effort. Contextual effects are directly proportional to relevance, while processing capability is inversely proportional to relevance. Processing effort is understood as the brainpower consumed in cognizing the language environment. The stronger the relevance, the more direct the discourse, and the less brainpower is consumed in cognition, resulting in a smaller cognitive load for the listener, and vice versa. In communication, the speaker's use of cognitive load increase and decrease manifests as the use of a communicative strategy.

The two main principles of Relevance Theory are: The first principle of relevance, the cognitive principle, posits that human cognition tends to maximize relevance. The second principle of relevance, the communicative principle, posits that every ostensive communicative act conveys a presumption that the act itself has optimal relevance. While distinguishing between the cognitive and communicative principles of relevance, Sperber and Wilson also differentiated between maximum and optimal relevance. The cognitive principle of relevance concerns maximum relevance, which belongs to the cognitive domain; the communicative principle of relevance concerns optimal relevance, which belongs to the communicative domain. He Ziran and Ran Yongping (1998) further pointed out that maximum relevance refers to achieving the maximum contextual effect with the minimum processing effort, while optimal relevance refers to obtaining adequate contextual effects after making effective effort in understanding discourse. Human cognition often aligns with maximum relevance, while communication expects to generate optimal relevance.

Due to cultural differences in customs, geography, humanistic knowledge between China and the West, we inevitably face difficulties in understanding English idioms. This section mainly aims to use the principles of maximum relevance, optimal relevance, etc., in the Relevance Theory to further understand and analyze the connotations of English idioms.

Some English idioms are conventional and carry rich cultural connotations. They possess the characteristic of being semantically integral and indissociable. The basis upon which the meaning of an idiom arises is a whole, and the true meaning can't be deduced from the literal meaning of the words. When understanding these types of idioms, no matter how much effort the listener puts into inferring in any given context, they may struggle to achieve the optimal relevance effect, hence failing to achieve the communicative purpose. Therefore, understanding the cultural connotation of the idiom and adopting a conventional translation method are required to understand the implied meaning of English idioms. For example:

1) A: What's your opinion?

B: We must try to solve the problem even if it is really a Gordian knot.

The idiom "A Gordian Knot" comes from ancient Greek mythology, which literally translates to "the knot of Gordius," and metaphorically signifies a "complex problem or challenge." The meaning of sentence B is "Even if it's a real tough problem, we should try to solve it." For person A, if they don't understand this idiom, it would be difficult for them to link "the knot of Gordius" with "complex problem or challenge," making it tough to achieve the contextual effect that the speaker intends to convey, thus failing to achieve the optimal relevance effect.

2) A: I crashed my father's car.

　　B: I'm sorry to her that. But you'd better tell your father what happened and face the music.

The literal meaning of the idiom "face the music" mentioned in B, which is "to confront music", is far from the actual meaning of "to take responsibility and face reality". There is no apparent connection between the two. Even in a hypothetical context to create such a relationship, person A would find it difficult to comprehend the message person B wants to convey. In other words, person A would struggle to infer the meaning of "having the courage to accept responsibility", and thus find it hard to achieve optimal relevance.

3) A: Tonight is my debut.

　　B: I hope you break a leg.

The literal meaning of the idiom "break a leg" is " a leg is made broken", but it actually signifies "wishing good luck and success in a performance". The meaning of "a leg is made broken" and "wishing good luck and success in a performance" are very disparate, and without understanding the cultural background, it's hard for a listener to imagine the true meaning of this idiom. Even in a certain context, it's challenging to fully comprehend the connotations of this idiom, which means that it's difficult for the listener to infer the speaker's communicative intention from the context, thus achieving optimal communication effectiveness.

4) A: John, why don't you meet your old flame anymore? You are frightened by your wife's punishment, right?

B: Stop pulling my legs. I have already been on the ropes.

The idiom "pull my legs" literally means "to pull someone's legs", but it has an extended meaning of "to joke with someone". It's hard for the listener to connect the literal meaning with the extended meaning, thus it's challenging to achieve maximum relevance and optimal relevance.

Despite the significant cultural differences between East and West, there are also many similarities. From a semantic perspective, English idioms exhibit a duality in their meanings. This duality refers to the literal and idiomatic meanings of English idioms. The literal meaning and the idiomatic meaning of an idiom can be vastly different, and in many cases, one must rely on contextual information to determine whether the phrase expresses its literal or idiomatic meaning. There are many English idioms that are analyzable; to understand these idioms, one simply needs to deduce the idiomatic meaning based on the literal meaning to achieve optimal relevance and grasp the speaker's intended communicative effect. For example:

5) A: I'm taking the final exam tomorrow.

B: Don't worry, honey. You've been learning so hard these days that the exam must be in the bag for you.

The idiomatic meaning of "in the bag" is "a sure thing, inevitable", completely different from its literal meaning. For speaker A to understand speaker B, they simply need to deduce the meaning of "in the bag". Literally, it indicates "something in your bag", which can easily lead to the understanding of "a sure thing, inevitable".

6) A: I always saw Nancy in your house. Is she a friend of your daughter?

B: Yes, she and Tina are very good friends. They are always

neck and neck in study, and they both like playing tennis and listening to the music.

One can imagine that if two people's necks are at the same height, their overall height must be similar. Thus, it's easy to understand that "neck and neck" is used to describe a situation where two people are in a closely matched or evenly balanced state. Speaker A can deduce the meaning of what speaker B said from the context, thus achieving optimal communicative effectiveness.

7) A: You are a wolf in sheep's clothing! Go out!

B: Don't be mad at me. You know it's Mary who made you so angry. And actually, I'm a goat.

The idiom "a wolf in sheep's clothing" literally means "a wolf dressed in sheep's skin". Through the context, speaker B can easily deduce the real meaning conveyed by this idiom, which is "a villain, a hypocrite".

8) A: Would you please help me out? The whole room is messed up by the party last night.

B: I will help you if you can give me a hand with homework. You scratch my back and I'll scratch yours.

The idiom "scratch my back and I'll scratch yours" in the conversation is a very vivid and interesting phrase. If your back itches and you can't reach it, it's best to have someone help you. Its literal meaning is "if you scratch my back, I'll scratch yours". Through the context, the listener can infer the meaning of this idiom, which is "if someone helps you, you should also look for opportunities to help them; mutual assistance". The listener can infer its underlying meaning in this context, achieving optimal communication effect.

Inevitably, a large number of English idioms will appear in the process of verbal communication. The above analysis of English idioms under the framework of speech act theory, conversational implication theory, and relevance theory can help us further understand the various pragmatic meanings and values of the rich cultural connotations reflected by English idioms in the process of verbal communication.

6 Multidimensional Classification of English Idioms

In English, idioms play a special and significant role, and they are widely used in daily life communication. The study of idioms has always been a hot topic among linguists, and different linguists have different perspectives on the study of idioms, thus defining them differently. There are many ways to classify English idiom, and different classification criteria yield different results.

He Renfang (1989) classified idioms into five categories according to the meanings of each component and their various relationships: combination idioms, association idioms, fusion idioms, idioms between combination and association, and idioms between association and fusion.

Wang Rongpei (2000) divided idioms into nine categories from the linguistic perspective: thematic classification method, communicative function classification method, semantic clarity classification method, syntactic function classification method, structure classification method, subject classification method, domain classification method, etymology classification method, and type classification method, then further subdivided idioms according to each classification method.

Ma Lidong (2014) classified English-Chinese non-equivalent idioms into three types: partially equivalent idioms, pseudo-equivalent idioms, and zero equivalent idioms.

Ferande (1996) classified idioms into: pure idioms, semi-idioms, and literal idioms; Cacciari, C. & P. Tabossi (1991, 1993) classified idioms from the perspective of transparency into transparent idiom and opaque idiom; Laufer (2000) classified idioms from the perspective of second language acquisition into total formal similar idiom, partial formal similar idiom, idiom with different semantic and formal structures but sharing the same conceptual metaphor as in L1 idioms, and idioms that neither exist semantically nor formally in L1 idioms.

Based on previous research, this chapter further explores the classification of English idioms from four perspectives: syntax, semantics, pragmatics, and culture.

6.1 Classification From the Syntactic Perspective

Broadly speaking, idiom refers to all habitual usage and special expression in a national language, which could be a word, a phrase or a sentence. An English idiom is made up of two or more words and possess its own unique syntactic structure. In the process of understanding and learning idioms, learners should understand and analyze the syntactic structure and grammatical functions of idioms. According to the grammatical function and structure of idioms, idioms can be divided into the following five types: noun idioms, adjective idioms, verb idioms, adverbial idioms, and sentence idioms. Chinese scholars Wen Xu and Chen Zhi' an (2005) believed that there are five types of English phrasal verbs: intransitive verb + adverb, intransitive verb + preposition, intransitive verb + adverb + preposition, transitive verb + adverb, and transitive verb + noun + preposition. In this regard, Cowie et al. (1992) proposed that "English idioms can be divided into predicate phrases and non-predicate phrases based on grammatical function and structural components, among which predicate phrases can be divided into verb + complement, verb + object, verb + object + complement, verb + indirect object + direct object, verb + object +

modifier; non-predicate phrases idioms can be further divided into noun phrases, adjective phrases, preposition phrases, adverb phrases, and repetition word phrases." The ideas put forward by Cowie et al. are used as further examples to illustrate the classification of English idioms from a syntactic point of view.

6.1.1 Predicate Phrases

In English, predicate phrases are the most common idioms. It centers on a verb and pair with other verbs, playing the role of predicate in a sentence. Predicate phrases can be further subdivided into verb + complement, verb + object, verb + object + complement, verb + indirect object + direct object, and verb + object + modifier.

6.1.1.1 The Structure of "Verb + Complement"

Examples of English idioms with the structure of "verb + complement" include the following:

be half the battle
be loud in one's praise
be three sheets in the wind
be sent to the block
be the cat's pajamas
be no great shakes
be no oil painting
be a devil to work
bend over backward
bolt to the bran
bleed to death
bolt upright
bolt down

dice with death
doss down
draw ahead
cool down
come true
come clean
fall into despair
fall short
feel the part
get uptight
get even with
go off the boil
go on a blind
go to the bottom
go to the deuce
go round the bend
go blue in the face
grasp for breath
make a clean breast of
make a bad break
make bold with
make no doubt
prove too hot to handle
put to death
search to the bottom
wear thin

6.1.1.2 The Structure of "Verb + Object"

Examples of English idioms with the structure of "verb + object" include the following:

addle one's brain
achieve one's end
bate one's breath
blow one's cover
burn one's fingers
burn the midnight oil
burn one's boats
bury the hatchet
blow one's top
box one's ears
blear sb.'s eye
burst one's boiler
break one's fall
break one's neck
break the spell
break the ice
catch sb.'s fancy
click one's heels
cool one's heels
cook the books
catch sb.'s eye
cry wolf
count one's chicken
cut one's own throat

cut the mustard
dedicate one's life
do one's nut
do one's duty
draw sb.'s fire
drive a hard bargain
darken sb.'s door
draw blood
drive a hard bargain
drive home
earn one's keep
eat humble pie
eat one's dinners
explore a myth
get one's blue
follow one's bent
feel the draught
fit/foot the bill
find one's feet
face the music
face the knocker
fly the flag
get a double take
get someone's goat
get the kick
get the knock
get the lead
gild the lily

give sb. his leave
hand ab a lemon
hold the floor
hold one's horses
hold the ring
hump one's bluey/swag
hump one's drum
jump the gun
jump the queue
keep the ring
keep one's legs
know the ropes
know one's onions
know one's distance
know one's own mind
lace sb.'s jacket
leave school
lose one's breath
lose one's block
lose the thread
marry money
make a killing
meet one's death
meet one's end
make joy
make the scene
miss the boat
move heaven and earth

open the ball
open Pandora's box
open the floodgates
offend the ear
pass the buck
pull the plug
pocket one's pride
pound one's ear
practice the law
pick one's brains
reach the ear
rally the troops
rap sb.'s knuckles
raise Cain
raise a laugh
raise the mischief
read sb.'s mind
rush one's fences
save one's breath
see double
strike a lead
shoot one's bolt
sail one's own boat
salt a mine
slip sb.'s mind
see service
sell the pass
settle one's affairs

shed crocodile tears
show one's hand
sooth the savage
sow the dragon's teeth
stay the course
strike a chord
strike gold
sweat blood
take air
take one's ease
take effect
take a drubbing
take a joke
take a powder
take the floor
take the plunge
take wing
take one's drop
toe the line
top one's boom
touch one's forelock
turn the corner
 try one's best
wind up one's bottom
wage one's law
turn sb.'s brain
use one's loaf
watch one's tongue

weave one's spell
wet one's whistle
wet the baby's head
whet ab's appetite
win the day
wring one's hands

6.1.1.3 The Structure of "Verb + Object + Complement"

Examples of English idioms with the structure of "verb + object + complement" include the following:

blood someone white
catch someone red-handed
catch sb. tripping
drive sb. round the bend
drive sb. to drink
drive sb. to suicide
drive someone mad
eat someone alive
find someone wanting
feed sb.'s sight
give sb. the air
give sb. the jink
give sb. a jump
give sb. the kick
get one's nose out of joint
keep sb. underfoot
give sb. the door

give sb. the cue
give sb. a drubbing
get something straight
kick sb. downstairs
kick sb. upstairs
kill something stone dead
lay the butter on
let the cat out of the bag
leave someone standing
milk someone dry
play sb. dirt
put sb. in the cart
put sb. at his ease
put the record straight
send someone crazy
send sb. packing
send sb. sprawling
show sb. the door
see sb. through difficulties
serve sb. right
shake someone rigid
stop something stone dead
sweep the board clean
sprawl one's last
take sb. standing

6.1.1.4 The Structure of "Verb + Indirect Object+ Direct Object"
Examples of English idioms with the structure of "verb + indirect

object+ direct object" include the following:

do sb. an injustice
of sb. in favor
do sb. a good turn
do someone credit
drop someone a line
deal someone a blow
give the devil his due
give sb. the hoof
give sb. the jim-jams
give sb. the slip
give sb. the jink
give someone the tip
give sb. the jumps
give sb. a kick
give sb. a show
give someone a big hand
give someone a rough ride
keep sb. company
lead sb. one
sell someone a pup
show someone a clean pair of heels
send her victorious
spin someone a yarn

6.1.1.5 The Structure of "Verb + Object+ Modifier"
Examples of English idioms with the structure of "verb + object+

modifier" include the following:

> avoid something like the plague
> blow something sky-high
> burn the candle at both ends
> carry something too far
> cast one's net wide
> follow sb. like a shadow
> have sth. at one's tongue's end
> get a kick out of sth.
> send sb. on a fool's errand
> hold sb. in high esteem
> know sth./sb. from A to Z
> need something like a hole in the head
> keep ab at arm's length
> keep sb. on the hop
> put sb. one his honour
> put one's foot in one's mouth
> put sb. through the hoop
> put sb. on the shake
> take the shine out of
> take something hard
> throw cold water over something
> trip the light fantastic
> wear one's learning lightly

6.1.2 Non-Predicate Phrases

English idioms in the non-predicate phrase structure primarily includes noun phrases, adjective phrases, preposition phrases, adverb phrases, and repetitive or contrasting phrases.

6.1.2.1 Noun Phrase Structure Idioms

The key word or central word in these types of idioms is a noun, which can function as a noun in a sentence. For example:

>a bad apple
>a close call
>a cold fish
>a dead duck
>a dog's death
>a double cross
>a doubting Thomas
>a drop in the bucket
>a dog in the manger
>a feather in one's cap
>a feast for the eyes
>a fly in the ointment
>a fly on the wheel
>a false dawn
>a gay dog
>a grass widow
>a guiding star
>a good mixer
>a home bird
>a hard nut
>a horse of another color
>a hen-pecked husband

a lone wolf
a lion in the path
a moot point
a vicious circle
a wet blanket
a whited sepulcher
a willing horse
a wolf in sheep's clothing
an apple of discord
Adam's apple
apple of one's eye
Arab of the gutter
back-seat driver
black dog
bird dog
big dog
blue devils
brownie points
brain trust
blue chip
book club
cat's paw
cold shoulder
crunch time
copy cat
dead cat
dirty dog
dead pan

Dutch courage
Dutch auction
king's weather
flesh and blood
forbidden ground
fond dream
hot dog
high tea
high colour
lazy dog
main drag
pink tea
red dog
rank and file
red herring
red tape
sad dog
sheet anchor
the apple of one's eye
the lion's share
the third degree
the widow's cruse
the writing on the wall
the upper crust
the white feather
third wheel
under dog
wear and tear

water dog
white elephant
wolf whistles
yellow dog

6.1.2.2 Adjective Phrase Structure Idioms

An adjective phrase structure idiom functions as an adjective in a sentence, but its constituent parts may not all be adjectives. For example:

all Greek
alive and kicking
as stiff as a poker
as busy as a bee
as cool as a cucumber
as meek as a lamb
as cool as a cucumber/ bread-and-butter
as poor as a church mouse
as white as a sheet
as strong as a horse
be fishy
big as saucers
black and blue
bone idle
clear cut
dead from the neck up
dead to the wide
free and easy
fleet of foot

flat as mustard
free and easy
green-eyed
green as grass
high and mighty
hot under the collar
home and dry
hungry as a hunter
high and mighty
long in the tooth
much of a muchness
null and void
on the go
on call
out of sorts
proud as Lucifer
quick as lightning
smooth as a pebble
so near and yet so far
sound in wind and limb
sound as a bell
thick s thieves
thin as a lath
touchy as hell
true as steel
vain as a peacock
wide of mark
wet behind the ears

white-collar
white-livered
white as a sheet
worth one's salt

6.1.2.3 Adverbial Phrase Structure Idioms

An adverbial phrase structure idiom functions as an adverb in a sentence. For example:

full in the face
full steam ahead
heart and soul
tooth and nail
hammer and tongs
hands down
hand in glove
here and there
here below
like a cat on hot bricks
like a fly in amber
until death us do part

6.1.2.4 Prepositional Phrase Structure Idioms

An prepositional phrase structure idiom functions as a preposition in a sentence. For example:

above one's bend
above all

after all
at your service
at wit's end
at any price
at first blush
between the scene
between the devil and the deep blue sea
between you and me
beyond all measure
by no means
by and by
by and large
by the way
by any means
by a whisker
by fair means of foul
by the same token
by virtue of something
for the birds
for dear life
from space to space
from pillar to post
in one's shoes
in the books
in one's book
in the black
in the pink
in a breeze

in any case
in the air
in the long run
like a cat with nine lives
like a dog with two tails
like a ship without a rudder
like water off a duck's back
of good standing
of the first magnitude
off the hook
off one's own bat
off the record
on the air
on an even keel
on one's toe
on the dame page
on tap
on the home front
out of the blue
on false pretences
out of the woods
out of thin air
out of alignment
off the press
over my dead body
through thick and thin
under cover of something
under someone's nose

under the wire
under the counter
with an air of
with all souls
with flying colors
with might and main
with one's back to the wall
without a hitch
without fear or favor
without prejudice

6.1.2.5 Repetitive or Contrasting Phrase Structure Idioms

There are some idiomatic expressions with repetitive or contrasting phrase structure. For example:

odds and ends
a man and a mouse
body and soul
bread and circuses
cash and carry
cut and dry
dead and alive
dust and ashes
end to end
fame and fortune
flesh and blood
fair and square
fit and proper

guns or butter
far and wide
first and last
high and dry
head to tail
heart to heart
here and now
law and order
loud and long
near and dear
milk and water
off and on
rough and ready
safe and sound
sugar and spice
sweetness and light
the cut and thrust
the ups and downs
tit for tat
twists and turns
through and through
wear and tear
wind and weather
wet or fine
well and truly
wit and wisdom
word or sign
wheeling and dealing

6.1.3 Sentence-Based Idioms

A sentence-based idiom is an omitted or complete sentence. It mainly appears in the form of proverb, aphorism, etc. In terms of sentence type, there are declarative sentences, interrogative sentences, imperative sentences, and exclamatory sentences. From the perspective of simple and complex sentences, there are simple sentences, compound sentences, and complex sentences. For example:

> A good beginning is half done.
> Better late than never.
> All men by nature desire knowledge.
> A fall into the pit, a gain in your wit.
> Better to do well than to say well.
> Better an egg today than a hen tomorrow.
> Care and diligence bring luck.
> Deeds are fruits; words are but leaves.
> Don't put the cart before the horse.
> Easier said than done.
> Every second counts.
> Good advice is beyond price.
> God helps those who help themselves.
> Haste makes waste.
> He that travels far knows much.
> Homer sometimes nods.
> Learn the new by reviewing the old.
> Nothing is difficult to a willing mind.
> Never do things by halves.

Man can conquer nature.
Man proposes and God disposes.
One today is worth two tomorrows.
One should eat to live, not live to eat.
Pain past is pleasure.
Practice makes perfect.
Reason is the guide and light of life.
Second thoughts are best.
Strike while the iron is hot.
Still waters run deep.
The leopard cannot change its spots.
Truth never grows old.
More than enough is too much.
What we see we believe.
When one door shuts, another opens.
You cannot eat your cakes and have them.
Youth is the season of hope.

6.2 Classification From the Semantic Perspective

From a semantic point of view, the meaning of an idiom is not the sum of the meanings of its components. Nunberg (1978, 1994) divided idioms into decomposable idioms, irregularly decomposable idioms, and indecomposable idioms. Cacciari and Tabossi (1991, 1993) divided idioms into transparent idioms and opaque idioms based on the degree of idiom transparency. Fernando (1996) classified idioms into three categories: pure idioms, semi-idioms, and literal idioms. Based on Fernando's views, further examples of English idioms will be provided.

6.2.1 Pure Idioms

An pure idiom refers to conventional compound word and collocation, where the original meaning is not discernible from its constituent parts and they do not express literal meaning. For example, "Lazy Susan" (a turntable): When many people hear "Susan", they immediately think of Auntie Susan, who is well-known throughout Britain. She quickly gained popularity on Britain's famous program "Got Talent," becoming a household name worldwide. However, the "Lazy Susan" mentioned here has nothing to do with Auntie Susan. It is said that a waitress named Susan in an American restaurant, who was too lazy to refill dishes for guests, designed a kind of round turntable placed at the center of the dining table. Diners only need to gently turn the turntable to get the dishes they want to eat. Since then, this kind of turntable has been used and named "Lazy Susan." Other examples of this type of idiom include the following:

ace in the hole
apple and orange
apple of discord
ask for the moon
backseat driver
go bananas
give it a shot
meet one's Waterloo
once in a blue moon
pull one's leg
shake a leg
tell me about it

walk one's chalks
Where's the beef?
white elephant
white war
zero in on

6.2.2 Semi-Idioms

A semi-idiom is a compound phrase where at least one component is a non-literal expression, with the literal meaning making up half of the overall idiomatic meaning. For example, "Jack of all trades" (proficient in many areas): Jack is a very common male name in English, used here to refer to any person, much like "John Doe" in English or "Zhang San, Li Si" in Chinese. Besides referring to trading, "trade" can also mean industry or profession. A person who knows various professions is, of course, proficient in many areas. Other examples of this type of idiom include the following:

all-nighter
a white soul
burn the midnight oil
black tea
cast sheep's eyes
blue film/story/joke
catch fire
Dutch courage
green house greenhouse
eat like a wolf
green revolution

go in one ear and out the other
foot the bill covers the cost
fat chance: small chance
happy as a clam is incomparable
in the same boat
kill the goose that laid the golden egg
mad as a hatter is crazy
man of straw
out of one's mind
out of time is out of place
put oil on the flames
yellow Book

6.2.3 Literal Idioms

A literal idiom refers to the fixed, variation-limited compound phrase, the meaning of which is the sum of the meanings of its components. For example:

a wolf in sheep's clothing
at first
at the foot of
after all
by and by
by no means
first and last
here and now
here and there
for example

in sum
in order to
off and on
on foot
on the top of
on the bottom of
so far
very important person

6.3 Classification From the Pragmatic Perspective

Pragmatics is a major branch of linguistics that primarily studies the meanings expressed by language in context. British linguist Seid (1978) once said, "English has a rich array of idioms, which are indispensable parts of the overall vocabulary. In fact, it's challenging to speak or write English without using idioms." It's evident that idioms and language are inseparable, and idioms play a significant role and function in English usage. Halliday, a representative figure of the systemic functional linguistics school, had a significant influence on the study of the pragmatic functions of English idioms. He proposed the three major metafunctions of language: ideational, interpersonal, and textual functions.

This provides a new theoretical perspective for a deeper understanding and comprehension of the nature, rules, and functions of language. Australian linguist Fernando (2000) applied Halliday's three metafunctions to study the role of language in communication and provided a comprehensive explanation of the ideational, interpersonal, and textual functions of idioms. She classified idioms based on different language functions into ideational idiom, interpersonal idiom, and relative idiom. This chapter, based on the summary and analysis of the ideational, interpersonal, and textual functions of English idioms and in accordance with Fernando's viewpoint, categorizes English idioms into three major types: ideational idioms, interpersonal idioms, and relational idioms, and further explicates them.

6.3.1 Ideational Idioms

Ideational function refers to the capability of language to express various experiences and internal activities in the real world. Although Halliday said that the three metafunctions of language exist simultaneously and are equally important, some linguists believe that among these three metafunctions, ideational function is the most crucial. Idioms are semantically holistic, and all forms of idioms can reproduce any social and psychological experiences of the objective and subjective world through the speaker's choice. It could be said that ideational function is the primary function of idioms.

Fernando believed that ideational idioms could convey a description of the impressions of the physical, social, and emotional world within a language community. Luo Shiping (2006) pointed out that ideational idioms, as a main component of idioms, can not only convey various information semantically and help language users express their subjective impressions of the world, but also describe behavior intentionally and metaphorically.

Peng Qinghua (2007) believed that "the ideational function of English idioms differs from the ideational function of general vocabulary. It is metaphorical and socio-cultural." When describing the objective and subjective world, English idioms make the language more concrete, vivid, and interesting through rhetorical devices like metonymy, personification, metaphor, and hyperbole. For example:

1) "heart and soul"

the literal meaning is the core part of a life, metaphorically signifying "wholeheartedly".

2) "go up in smoke"

the literal meaning is "to turn into smoke" and is extended to mean "everything goes in vain, all efforts are wasted".

3) "under my roof"

It metaphorically means "my home". Roof is used metonymically here, signifying the house, a part representing the whole. Similar expressions including "go under the hammer" "hard on someone's heels" "lose one's nerve" "long in the tooth", etc.

4) In English culture, people are often likened to "dogs," hence there are many idioms about "dogs", such as dog-eat-dog (ruthless), lucky dog (fortunate person), sea dog (seasoned sailor), dog days (holidays), lead a dog's life (to live a life of poverty), top dog (person in charge, leader), every dog has its day (everyone gets a chance).

Below are some English idioms that have ideational functions:

Achilles' heel
as snug as a bug in a rug
a real peach
big wheel
between the devil and the deep blue sea
birds of a feather flock together.
couch potato
black sheep
drink like a fish

every cloud has a silver lining
fifth wheel
give it a shot
hit the nail on the head
in the doghouse
let one's hair down
make bricks without straw
odd fish
with flying colors

Ideational idioms leave a deep impression on people, the information they convey is specific and clear, providing various information that the topic wants to express, with a high amount of information. Most English idioms belong to ideational idioms and are widely used in all aspects of people's lives, such as speeches, books, magazines, radio, television, internet, etc.

1) English idioms from family life:

bread and butter
bring the house down
earn one's bread
butter up
whole cheese
money for jam

2) English idioms from sports and entertainment:

behind the eight ball

have a game plan
down and out
put all one's cards on the table
rain check
slam dunk
play the field
jump the gun
pull one's weight
bet one's bottom dollar
sweep the board
back to square one
fall guy
make a pig of oneself

3) English idioms from nautical life:

be in the same boat
sink or swim
rest on one's oars
high water mark
all at sea
in full sail

4) English idioms from education:

A child's life is like a piece of paper on which every person leaves a mark.
A pet lamb makes a cross ram.

A man that begets a barren cannot have a grandchild.
A painful experience makes us cautious in the future.
Mother's darlings are but milksop heroes.
No sweet without some sweat.
Praise the young and they will blossom.

6.3.2 Interpersonal Idioms

Interpersonal function refers to how speakers use language to interact with others, establish and maintain interpersonal relationships, influence others' behavior with language, express their views of the world, and even change it. Peng Qinghua (2007) proposed that the interpersonal function of English idioms is primarily reflected in the following aspects: promoting interaction between the speaker and listener; adhering to the principle of politeness in conversation; establishing and maintaining friendly interpersonal relationships through conventional greetings in daily life; expressing the speaker's varying attitudes and tones towards different people or matters, thereby influencing or persuading others in communication. Chang Chenguang (2004) pointed out that English idioms are an important resource for expressing interpersonal meaning, playing a crucial role in both demonstrating interactions between communicators and expressing the speaker's personal attitudes and evaluations.

Fernando believes that the primary function of most idiomatic expressions is communication, and idioms with interpersonal features serve as tags of politeness or friendliness in daily communication. Examples include "How do you do?" "How are you?" "May I speak to ..., please." "Do you mind if I use your phone?" "Have a good time!" etc. Idioms are an important part of language and its practical use, embodying rich cultural and pragmatic meanings. Establishing friendly relationships in communication is a vital foundation for people to acquire information, thus people must adhere to the pragmatic principles that should be observed during the process. Let's study the practical application of idioms in interpersonal communication.

1) When people meet, they often greet each other with phrases expressing greetings, apologies, wishes, etc. These sentences have become conventional in communication.

For example:

> How do you do?
> Nice to meet you.
> How are you?
> I am fine, thank you. And you?
> Excuse me.
> How's everything going?
> What's up?
> Have a good time!
> How is everything?
> Good luck to you.
> May you both be happy!
> May they live long!
> Long may he live!
> May she enjoy her life!
> Have a good time!
> Can I help you?
> God bless you!

2) In the process of interpersonal communication, people often use some English idioms that express emotions, such as expressing surprise, joy, anger, and irritation.

For example:

> It's a big surprise!
> Oh, my God.
> You crap.
> I hate his guts.
> I am just ecstatic about going to visit you soon.
> You make me sick.
> I know he has the blues, but it doesn't mean he can vent his anger on me.
> That is going too far.
> Stop playing the food.
> Don't act stupid.
> Thank God it's Friday.
> Good business!
> Goodness me.
> It really sucks.
> Here we go.

3) Idiomatic expressions of intent in English, such as idioms expressing "pleading, proposing, suggesting, ordering, instructing, warning, threatening" and other actions.

For example:

> Who do you think you're talking to?

Don't get fresh with me.
It's none of your business.
Mind your own business.
Who asked you?
Do I look like a fool?
Who do you think I am?
What kind of a fool do you take me for?
This is for your ears only.
This is just between you and me.
This doesn't leave this room.
Do it yourself then.
That is more like it.
You wit the rail on the head.
See I told you so.
I'm counting on you.
I wasn't born yesterday.
Who do you think you are?
What do you think you are doing?
How goes the enemy?
How dare you talk to me like that?
Make my day.
Stay away, if you know what's good for you.
Where do we go from here/ there?
Back to square one.
What are we waiting for?
How's about a drink?
Why not do it?

6.3.3 Relational Idioms

A single sentence or a sentence fragment often cannot complete language communication. To form a coherent discourse, relational idiom is a must. Relational idiom is the medium of logical semantics and time coherence in the text, making the various parts of the text connected. Relational idiom is fixed in structure and semantics, including words, phrases, and sentences. As a means of lexical cohesion, relational idiom provides language users with a ready-made resource for connecting words and phrases. It is "pre-fabricated expression" of meaning, limited in number yet essential in function. According to Fernando, relational idiom is a tool for logical and temporal coherence in text. The importance of relational idioms is exemplified through the analysis of the following essay.

> It is of great significance for a college student to know the world outside the campus. In this fast-developing "Information Age", college students must keep pace with the progress of the world. <u>Additionally,</u> by contacting the off-campus world, college students can have chance to get more practical skills. <u>Therefore,</u> how to know the world outside the campus is worth our attention.
>
> Many ways can be adopted by our college students to increase our knowledge of the world. <u>Firstly,</u> mass media, such as radios, televisions, newspapers and the Internet, are a good choice, by which we can be well informed about what is happening. <u>Secondly,</u> providing volunteer services is an efficient way to contact and know the society. <u>Thirdly,</u> we can take part-time jobs to increase our practical experience.
>
> <u>As for me</u>, I will try to create and grasp more chances to

contact the society. In my opinion, getting to know the off-campus world is as important as improving academic performance. Therefore, I suggest every college student should not confine himself to the campus but often go outside.

The underlined words and phrases above all belong to related idioms, which can make the article clear and coherent. "additionally" and "therefore" are used to bring up the previous text and foreshadow the following text. In addition to indicating the semantic relationship between the previous and the following, these two phrases also allow the listener to recall the content mentioned in the context, and at the same time predict the development and outcome of the following text. This category of idioms also includes "in addition" "quite the reverse" "as a result of" "besides" "to conclude" , etc. "Firstly" "Secondly" and "Thirdly" are used to indicate the temporal order and the time frame of the event. This category of idioms also includes "once upon a time" "time out of mind" "all the year round" "for good and all" "all of a sudden" "less than no time" , etc.

"As for me" is a relative idiom that introduces personal opinions. There are also some relative idioms for introducing someone's opinion or different opinions, such as "as far as I am concerned" "when it comes to" "some people think/prefer to/ choose" "in one's opinion" "they maintain/ they point out", "I agree", etc.

This category of relative idioms such as "not ...but" often does not add new information, but it can make the semantics clear and coherent between the previous and the following. This category of idiom also includes "not only...but also" "seeing that" "on the one hand" "on the other hand" "on the contrary" "so that" "in order to" , etc.

6.4 Classification From the Cultural Perspective

Culture refers to the sum total of the spiritual and material civilization created by human beings through social and historical practices. It reflects every aspect of a nation's life and includes three dimensions: spiritual, social, and material. Language serves as the carrier of culture, and the use of language can fully reflect the culture of a region or nation. Idiom, as the essence of language, is imbued with rich cultural connotations. Understanding the cultural characteristics of English idioms can help us to gain insights into cultural information such as the society, customs, and way of life of English-speaking countries. This section explores English idioms from the spiritual, social, and material life.

6.4.1 English Idioms Related to Spiritual Life

Spiritual life includes religion, philosophy, science, art, etc. For example, religion is the spiritual force of Westerners, and God is their master. Christianity is the traditional belief of Westerners. Therefore, there are many idioms related to religion in English. For example:

Good God!
A man without religion is a horse without bridle.
The danger past and God forgotten.
God speed you!
Man proposes, God disposes.
Have God and have all.

Art is a reflection of people's thoughts, and English idioms related to art are:

The landscape belongs to the man who looks at it.

The love of beauty is an essential part of all healthy human nature.

The poet's voice need not merely be the record of man, it can be one of the props, the pillars to help him endure and prevail.

6.4.2 English Idioms Related to Social Life

Social life refers to the interaction, communication, and relationships among people in a community or society. It involves various forms of social connections, such as family, friends, peers, neighbors, coworkers, and acquaintances. Social life includes activities, such as socializing, attending events, participating in clubs or organizations, and engaging in leisure activities. It also encompasses social norms, values, and customs that guide social behavior and relationships. Social life is essential for human well-being, and it plays a significant role in shaping personal identity and social identity. There are many English idioms related to social life. Some English idioms are related to economics and politics, which is a part of social life. Some examples are illustrated as follows:

"Beat your swords into plowshares", which metaphorically means abandoning disputes in pursuit of peace, is frequently used in different social and political groups.

"Everything but the kitchen sink" meaning "everything possible", comes from the US military in World War II, where both sides would use all available weapons and manpower in fierce battles to win the war. Today, this idiom is widely used in various fields such as economics and entertainment, including political campaigns.

Other similar idioms include "jump on the bandwagon" "on the warpath" "power behind the throne" "make a federal case out of something" and "shoot from the hip".

As an island nation, Britain has a well-developed maritime industry, resulting in many English idioms related to ships and water, such as "a small leak will sink a great ship" "drink like a fish" "miss the boat" "sea dog" and "spend money like water".

Many American English idioms are related to historical allusions, using historical events to illustrate a lesson or describe a similar event, such as "according to Hoyle", meaning "according to custom" or "meet one's waterloo", which refers to a crushing defeat, referencing Napoleon's defeat at Waterloo. "Round-table conference" originated from the story of King Arthur organizing a group of brave knights to defend the country, with a large round table made to ensure the warriors' equal status with no distinctions of rank. Nowadays, it is often used to describe meetings where everyone has an equal voice. American English idioms reflect life in society, with many slang terms related to social life and culture, such as "smoker eater" "bad mouth" "pooped out" and "give him the air" among others. Different social groups often have their own specific circle of life, resulting in different slang used among different classes and regions. For example, among college students, "He is just a booker" means "he studies too much", while "You are out of your tree" means "you are out of your mind."

6.4.3 English Idioms Related to Material Life

Material life refers to the aspect of human existence that is focused on material possessions, physical needs, and the pursuit of material wealth. It is the pursuit of material goods and comforts, such as food, shelter, clothing, and other possessions necessary for survival and enjoyment. Material life is often characterized by consumerism, status-seeking, and competition for resources. It can be contrasted with spiritual life, which is focused on the pursuit of higher values, meaning, and purpose beyond the material world. Material life is an essential aspect of human survival.

As the saying goes, "food is the paramount necessity of the people", and food is closely related to human life. In English, there are many idioms related to food, such as "bread and circuses" which refers to small favors provided by the government to appease the people, originating from the famous satirist Juvenal's 10th satire which coined the phrase "panem et circenses" (bread and circuses). The term "bread and circuses" still means "food and entertainment" used by rulers to appease the people. Other idioms include "an egg-head" for knowledgeable people, "take the bread out of someone's mouth" for taking away someone's livelihood, "the salt of the earth" for pillars of society, "a hard nut to crack" for difficult problems or people, "have egg/jam on/over one's face" for feeling embarrassed, "a land flowing with milk and honey" for a prosperous place, "pie in the sky" for unrealistic plans, "sour grapes" for cynical remarks, "full of beans" for energetic or enthusiastic, and "salad days" for youthful and inexperienced.

Categorizing English idioms from syntax, semantics, pragmatics, and culture can help us better understand idiom and the cultural background of Western countries, thus improving our English.

7 English Idiom Comprehension From Four Perspectives

7.1 English Idiom Comprehension From the Syntactic Perspective

Based on the previous research, this section conducts a systematic study of English idioms from a syntactic perspective for college students, putting forward theoretical and practical suggestions for learning English idioms, aiming to help college students master idioms more effectively.

7.1.1 Classification of English Idioms From a Syntactic Point of View

From a syntactic perspective, idioms, as a special type of multi-word structure, have their unique syntactic structures. According to Cowie, English idioms can be divided into clause idioms and phrase idioms. Clause idioms can be further divided into five subcategories, namely: verb + complement; verb + direct object; verb + direct object + complement; verb + indirect object + direct object; verb + indirect object + adjunct. Phrase idioms can also be divided into five subcategories, namely: nominal phrases; adjectival phrases; prepositional phrases; adverbial phrases; phrases with repetition and contrastive elements. This syntactic classification is valuable. Students can classify idioms into these categories to organize the seemingly confusing and numerous idioms systematically. On the one hand, it helps students to memorize the spelling of idioms in bulk; on the other hand, it helps students to understand the grammatical function of idioms in sentences.

Students often make grammatical errors when using idioms in sentences, and the reason is that they ignore the syntactic classification of idioms. If the syntactic classification of idioms is correct, their grammatical function will be self-evident. For example:

1) Subordinate clause idioms

a. Verb + complement: turn on, go off, deteriorate, go to sleep, explode, come to life

b. Verb + direct object: keep one' s word, burn one' s boats, hit the books

c. Verb + direct object + complement: drive someone mad, call someone names

d. Verb + indirect object + direct object: give someone a big hand, drop someone a line

e. Verb + direct object + additional components: take something seriously, fit someone like a glove

2) Phrase idioms

a. Noun phrases: white elephant f, dark horse, a piece of cake

b. Adjective phrases: free and easy, as poor as a rat, up in the air, undecided

c. Preposition phrases: on the contrary, at the eleventh hour, to pit out

d. Adverbial phrases: heart and soul, behind closed doors, secretly, through thick and thin

e. phrases that include elements of repetition and contrast: hand in hand, day by day, diamond cut diamond

The classification of English idioms is helpful for students to understand and master these idioms. When encountering English idioms, students should analyze their syntactic structures and classify them into the aforementioned patterns. On one hand, the classification of idioms can help students sort out seemingly disordered idioms, which can facilitate memorizing a batch of idioms at once. On the other hand, as the grammatical functions of different sentence structures vary, it is beneficial for students to master the grammar usage in sentences. In fact, students often make grammatical errors in using idioms because they have no knowledge of the syntactic classification of idioms. Once using the syntax classification of idioms, their grammatical functions can be effectively verified.

Take the idiom "come to life" as an example. According to its syntactic structure, students should classify "come to life" into the pattern of verb phrase complement. Since "come to life" belongs to the clause-type idiom, it has some characteristics of a clause idiom. "Come to life" will act as the predicate verb complement pattern. Therefore, students can master the grammar usage of "come to life" and make a correct sentence, such as "The forest has come to life." If students make mistakes in analyzing the grammatical structure, they may create a wrong sentence, such as "The forest is come to life." The idiom "burn one's boats" is another good example. For most students, this is a very special idiom, which means "to burn one's bridges" in Chinese, a commonly known idiom for Chinese students. Here we can analyze the syntactic structure of English idioms, which is also the key to understanding and mastering them. "Burn" determines its syntactic structure as a verb. In fact, as a verb, the idiom "burn one's boats" should be classified as a pattern of verb-direct object, which acts as a direct object structure in a sentence. In addition to clause idioms, there are also phrase idioms, such as "a piece of cake," which can be classified as a noun idiom and are frequently used in our daily lives.

Understanding its usage is very practical for us. When students know that the idiom "a piece of cake" acts as a noun phrase, they can easily make sentences, such as "English is just a piece of cake."

In addition to noun phrase idioms, English idioms can also be classified as adjective phrase, prepositional phrase, adverb phrase, containing comparative and repetitive phrase idioms, which make many complicated English idioms more concise and clear. When we have mastered one category, we can quickly know its structural composition for the same category, which can help us easily understand related sentences or articles.

Therefore, highlighting the grammatical functions of idioms and conducting syntactic analysis of idioms is very important. Correct syntactic analysis can help second language learners master the grammatical habits of idioms, while ignorance or errors in syntactic analysis may result in the loss of second language learners. Syntactic analysis can facilitate students' understanding and acquisition of idioms.

7.1.2 Investigation and Experimental Study on College Students

7.1.2.1 Purpose, Subjects and Methods of the Survey

This section aims to understand the attitude of college students towards English idioms and the current situation of their mastery of idioms through a questionnaire survey of 55 students in Guangxi National Normal University, Guangxi Zhuang Autonomous Region.

55 students in Guangxi National Normal University, Guangxi Zhuang Autonomous Region are surveyed. When being surveyed, these 55 students said that although they had basically mastered a certain English vocabulary, they still did not understand English idioms. They translated those idioms only according to their literal meaning, and did not know their metaphorical meaning.

The study adopts a questionnaire survey and interview method, and it is divided into two parts. The first part is the idiom test, which mainly examines the students' mastery of idioms. The second part is the interview, which mainly focuses on examining how students acquire and master English idioms.

7.1.2.2 Questionnaire

The questionnaire mainly contains two aspects: a test on idioms and an interview with the students, with a total of 25 test questions, including 12 verb phrases, 3 noun idioms, 3 adjective idioms, 3 preposition idioms, 3 adverbial idioms, and 3 idioms including elements of repetition and contrast.

7.1.2.3 Data Analysis and Interview

The first question is to determine the scope of college students, and the subjects of this questionnaire are 55 first-year college students.

The second question is "Do you study English idioms in a targeted or systematic manner?"

Among the 55 students, only 6 have studied English idioms systematically, while the numbers of those who occasionally or almost never studied them are both 14. 21 students, the largest number, have not studied English idioms systematically. It is shown that only a very small proportion of students have specifically studied idioms, and the majority of them have not learned them purposefully.

A total of 55 college students were tested. From the chart 7-1 of English idiom test scores above, it can be seen that there is a large fluctuation in scores between students, indicating a significant difference in their English idiom proficiency. There are more students with scores from 30 to 60 points. The total score for the English Idioms test is 100 points, and only 8 students reached the passing line of 60 points, accounting for only 14.5% of the total number of students. This indicates that students in the tested class have very little knowledge of English idioms and very poor English idiom proficiency.

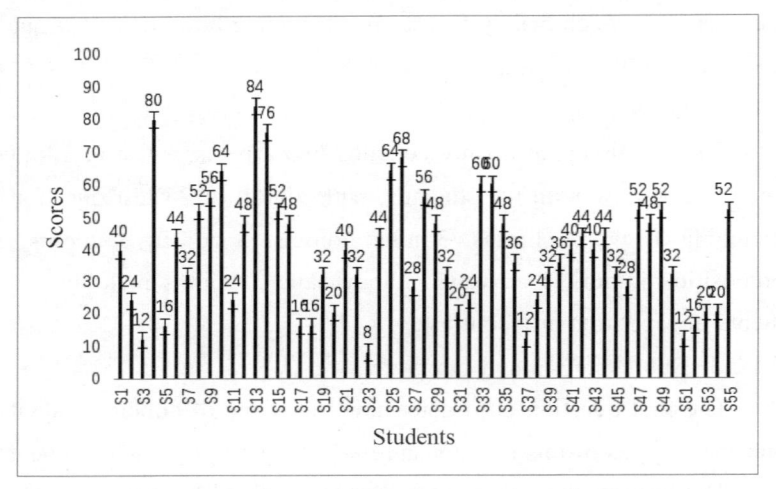

Chart 7-1 English Idiom Test Class Score

The maximum score of the 55 students in the English idioms test is 84, and the lowest score is 8. The average score of the class is only 38.91.

In brief, the study shows that there is a significant gap in terms of the subjects' proficiency in learning English idioms, and overall, the scores of the class's English idiom learning fall far below the passing line, which is a very worrying situation. In order to understand the origin and development of students' acquisition of English idioms, we conducted group interviews. Five students were randomly selected from these 55 students for the interview. The questions asked during the interview were: Do you think English idioms are important? Why or why not? How do you learn English idioms?

Regarding the first question, most of the interviewed students acknowledged the importance of English idiomatic expressions, particularly in writing and reading comprehension, because using appropriate idiomatic expressions in writing would make a teacher view one's work more favorably and result in higher scores. In reading comprehension, if a student is not familiar with an idiomatic expression, it could hinder their understanding of the article. As for the second question, the students gave various answers as follows:

Student A: I don't have a specific method. When I learn English, I try to memorize their spellings and meanings, which is similar to the Chinese method of rote memorization. I think idiomatic expressions are like words, so I use the same method.

Student B: I don't think idiomatic expressions are very important. I remember them if I can, but I don't study them specifically.

Student C: Idiomatic expressions are unique and sometimes different from words. For some idiomatic expressions, I mostly learn them by rote memorization, such as "turn on", "go off", and "black horse", each of which is a single unit, like a word. For some idiomatic expressions, I can relate them to other things. For example, "as poor as a rat" is an interesting idiom. When I saw it, I thought the literal meaning was that someone was as poor as a rat, but actually, it is a metaphorical idiom with the same meaning as a Chinese idiom "*yī pín rú xǐ*" indicating poverty. Most English idiomatic expressions seem similar to Chinese idioms but have completely different meanings, such as "hit the books," which literally means "to hit a book," but it metaphorically means "to study hard." Most idiomatic expressions are vague, so I think understanding English idiomatic expressions depends on cultural factors such as their background and origin.

Student D: I have been unable to find an effective method for learning English idiomatic expressions, which makes me feel helpless as English idiomatic expressions become increasingly important.

Student E: Learning idiomatic expressions by rote memorization is actually safe but very boring. We cannot remember so many things by just memorizing them. I tried to find some convenient and effective methods, but I failed. I think maybe there is no such method. Whenever I come across a new idiomatic expression, I have to look it up in a dictionary, which makes it difficult for me to concentrate on the story I am reading. I crave an effective method for learning idiomatic expressions.

7.1.2.4 Findings

From the content of the interview, we can make a summary of the situation of students' acquisition of English idioms: English idioms are important and should be valued; An idiom is like a word, which can be learnt by rote memorization; There is a need for an effective method for acquiring English idioms.

Based on tests and interviews, we can understand the current state of college students' understanding and acquisition of English idioms. Currently, the grasp of English idioms among college students is very worrying. Even though they understand the importance of English idioms, they cannot find an effective method and therefore have limited knowledge or even no understanding of them. Chinese college students face great difficulties in understanding and acquiring English idioms. They typically use traditional rote memorization methods when learning them. Additionally, they lack interest in English idioms and tend to avoid using them in verbal and written communication. They urgently need some new methods for acquiring English idioms.

7.1.3 Conclusion

Idiom is an important component of the vocabulary system in language, and various languages including English have a rich collection of idioms. For college students, learning English idioms is indispensable while studying English. The main focus of this research is on college students' understanding of English idioms from a syntactic point of view. Based on previous research, this research examine college students' comprehension of English idioms and provides new insights and ideas for teaching English idioms from a syntactic perspective.

This research has three theoretical implications. First, it helps deepen the understanding of the rules governing idioms and their important role in the language system. Second, it emphasizes that idiom acquisition is not simply a matter of word memorization, but follows internal rules. Third, it offers theoretical and pedagogical guidance for the acquisition and teaching of English idioms.

There are three aspects of practical significance. Firstly, it allows for college students to acquire English idioms from various perspectives and methods, especially the mastery of the rules of idiomatic expressions. Secondly, teachers need to guide students in analyzing the syntax structure of idioms and inferring their metaphorical meanings from the components of the idioms. Thirdly, it provides some suggestions for English learners to quickly and effectively master English idioms.

College English teaching should help students build a solid language foundation, grasp effective language learning methods, and improve their cultural literacy to prepare them for more advanced studies ahead. As the essence of the language, English idioms are widely used in all areas of English communication, and a correct understanding of English idioms is an essential foundation for listening, speaking, reading, writing and translation. Moreover, language is the carrier of culture, and English idioms are no exception. Therefore, the teaching of English idioms is an important way to achieve the goals of English teaching, and should play a vital role in English teaching. There are some suggestions for college English idiom teaching and learning.

   Teachers can use syntactic analysis methods to teach English idioms, classify idioms in textbooks and demonstrate the advantages of their grammatical functions, which not only help students find a way to learn English idioms, but also promote their understanding of English grammar. For English learners, it is important not to learn English idioms aimlessly but in a targeted and systematic way. Simply memorizing idioms can lead to low learning efficiency and poor results. Learners should learn to analyze the structure of English idioms and classify them, especially from the perspective of their grammatical functions, which is an effective method for acquiring idioms.

   The limitations of this research lie in its inability to cater to a more comprehensive and deeper understanding of college students' mastery of English idioms, as well as a thorough exploration of the syntactic rules of English idioms. It is hoped that through this research, college students can benefit and achieve further progress in their English idiom learning.

7.2 English Idiom Comprehension From the Semantic Perspective

7.2.1 Introduction

   Semantics provides us with a new perspective to explore the

semantics of idioms. Studying the features of English idioms and their understanding from a semantic point of view can deepen the understanding of linguistic rules, and provide theoretical and methodological guidance for Chinese students to understand and acquire idioms. This can effectively help English learners grasp the essence of idioms and their rules, enhance cross-cultural awareness, improve their pragmatic abilities, and ultimately enable learners to fully master and use English. Based on previous research and the actual situation of Chinese college students' acquisition of idioms, this research investigates college students' understanding of English idioms from a semantic perspective, which has both theoretical and practical significance.

7.2.2 The Semantic Characteristics of Idioms

Semantically, understanding and acquiring idioms requires understanding and acquiring the semantic meaning of idioms, which is metaphorical meaning, rather than literal meaning. The semantic meaning of idioms has three characteristics: holistic, transparency (decomposability), and specificity.

Holism is an important feature of idioms, which means that the meaning of idioms is an inseparable whole. Its semantic meaning does not simply add up the literal meanings of its constituent parts, but acquires a structural meaning from the combination of its constituent parts. The meaning of an idiom is a whole, which means that we must learn idioms as a whole. For example, "see red" means to get angry, and the meaning of the idiom has nothing to do with the literal meanings of the constituent words. Even if there are individual words or even several words that still retain their original meanings in many idioms, if they are not understood as a whole combination, the true meaning of the idiom cannot be correctly understood. Similar situations are countless in idioms. Therefore, the semantic wholeness is a semantic feature that is common to all idioms.

Transparency, also known as decomposability, refers to the contribution of the literal meaning of the constituent parts of idioms to the metaphorical meaning of the idiom as a whole. High transparency idioms have a very close connection between literal and metaphorical meanings, so it is relatively easy to infer the metaphorical meaning based on the literal meaning, such as the idioms "as blind as a bat" (almost blind) and "rain cats and dogs" (heavy rain). Low transparency idioms have a loose or no connection between literal and metaphorical meanings, making it difficult to infer the metaphorical meaning based on the literal meaning, such as the idioms "a wet blanket" (spoilsport) and "paint the town red" (celebrate wildly). However, idioms without any connection at all are rare, and most idioms can find corresponding connections between literal and metaphorical meanings.

Specificity is manifested in two forms: semantics that are illogical and semantics that cannot be analogized. Semantics that are illogical refer to some English idioms that are clearly deviating from logical thinking from the combination of words to semantics, but have been used continuously without any changes. For example, "grass widow" refers to a divorced, abandoned, or temporarily separated woman, and this idiom not only has illogical collocation of words, but also has a significantly different semantic meaning from the original meaning. Similarly, the idiom "There is no love lost between them" seems to be grammatically logical, but its idiomatic meaning is completely opposite to the literal meaning. In daily life, such illogical idioms are ubiquitous, such as "handsome is that" (true beauty lies in good behavior), "get someone's number" (see through someone's true nature), "neck and crop" (completely) and so on. Semantics that cannot be analogized refer to some idioms that cannot be changed, innovated, or misinterpreted by analogy, otherwise it is easy to misunderstand or misrepresent the idiom. For example, we cannot change "take in hand" to "take in hands" or "take into hand," cannot change "the last word" to "the last worlds," and cannot analogize "upside down" to "downside up," etc. They are unrelated to each other and in any case, we cannot use analogy to infer the unknown meaning of idioms, let alone use the known semantic meaning of idioms to change or create new idioms.

There are few studies of college students' understanding of English idioms from a semantic perspective. In view of this, this book attempts to study how college students acquire and understand English idioms from a semantic point of view. Studying the characteristics and understanding of English idioms from the perspective of semantics can deepen the understanding of language rules, provide theoretical and methodological guidance for Chinese college students to understand and acquire idioms, which can improve their pragmatic ability, and finally enable learners to deeply master and use English idioms.

7.2.3 An Empirical Study on English Idiom Comprehension Among College Students

7.2.3.1 Research Objectives and Significance

Based on previous research on idiom comprehension and acquisition, this study aims to investigate college students' comprehension of English idioms, and to analyze idiom features and comprehension from a semantic perspective. This can reveal the composition rules of idioms, deepen understanding of language rules, and provide theoretical and methodological guidance for Chinese students to understand and acquire idioms. Specifically, this study has the following objectives:

1) Investigate English idiom comprehension among college students.

2) Identify problems in the process of comprehending English idioms for college students.

Mastering scientific methodology is very important for college students to understand and learn English idioms, which can make them try to avoid mistakes when communicating in English and improve their English language communication skills. Understanding and learning English idioms from a semantic perspective has profound implications, including theoretical and practical significance:

1) Reveal the great role of semantic analysis in understanding English idioms, and provide theoretical and methodological guidance for Chinese college students to understand and acquire English idioms.

2) Make both teachers and students realize that idiom acquisition is not based on rote memorization, but has internal regularity.

3) Provide new ideas for teaching English idioms to improve teaching efficiency.

7.2.3.2 Research Methods

1) Subjects

The main subjects of this study are 50 students from Guangxi National Normal University, Guangxi Zhuang Autonomous Region. The reasons for choosing them as subjects are mainly based on three factors. Firstly, they have a certain amount of English vocabulary and skills in understanding English idioms due to more than six years of learning English. Secondly, they will face the challenge of the college English test band 4 or 6. But currently, their comprehension and acquisition of English idioms is poor. So, they urgently need correct methodologies to guide their comprehension and mastery of English idioms and improve their English language. Finally, because many English teachers are not aware of the importance for understanding and mastering English idioms from a semantic perspective, they rarely or even do not teach students some methods related to semantic analysis. This results in students ignoring the necessity of semantic analysis, making the comprehension of English idioms more difficult.

2) Research Instrument

a. Questionnaire

This questionnaire asks subjects to translate some English idioms into Chinese to examine college students' comprehension of English idioms. The total score of the questionnaire is 100 points, with a total of 25 questions, each worth 4 points. Among them, there are 13 questions with high transparency idioms, and 12 questions with low transparency idioms. A total score above 90 is excellent, above 60 (including 60) is pass, and below 60 is failure.

b. Interview

Six students in the class will be randomly selected from the class for interviews in this survey. These six students are referred to as A, B, C, D, E, and F. The main purpose of the interview is threefold: first, to survey what methods college students adopt in their acquiring English idioms; second, to survey how college students comprehend English idioms; third, to identify what difficulties college students will encounter in the process of comprehending English idioms.

7.2.3.3 Research process

1) Data Collection of Questionnaire

After the researcher designs the content of the questionnaire, the questionnaire is distributed to students in class, one for each student, to be completed within 30 minutes. The researcher explains the purpose of this research and the questionnaire survey to the students, each student must answer honestly, and strictly follow the rules of the questionnaire survey. After all students in the class complete the questionnaire, the researcher collects all the questionnaires, carefully corrects all the questionnaires, and finally analyzes the data according to the students' questionnaire scores.

2) Data Collection of Interview

With the cooperation of the teacher in charge of the class, the researcher randomly interviews six students and explains the purpose of the interview. The students are told that the interview will not affect their exam scores, and they are encouraged to share their thoughts and opinions truthfully. During the interview, the researcher asks the following questions:

a. How do you usually acquire English idioms?

b. How do you comprehend English idioms?

c. What problems are you confronted with in comprehending English idioms?

These questions are designed to survey college students' ways of acquiring and comprehending English idioms and the difficulties they are confronted with in the process of understanding.

7.2.3.4 Results and Discussion

1) Results and discussion of the questionnaire

A total of 50 students were surveyed in the study, all of whom answered the questionnaire honestly. The researcher spent a week analyzing the data from the 50 questionnaires, carefully checking for accuracy.

The students' scores are shown in Table 7-1, which shows that only one student in the class scored over 90, two students scored 60-

89, and overall, three students scored above 60 (including 60), while 47 students scored below 60. The excellence rate of the class is 2%, and the passing rate is 6%. These data show that the students' excellence and passing rates are very low, and college students have great difficulties in understanding English idioms. They have not mastered scientific and reasonable strategies for acquiring and comprehending English idioms, and it is urgent for them to find the correct methods to improve their English skills.

Table 7-1 Student Scores

Fraction	Number	Percentage
≥90	1	2%
≥60	3	6%
<60	47	94%

According to the statistics of student responses, the accuracy rate for each question is shown in Table 7-2. The data shows that the highest accuracy rates are for questions 1, 16, 18, and 25. The idioms used in these questions are relatively transparent. For example, the idioms "long time no see" and "fat chance" are easy to understand and belong to the category of literal idioms without metaphorical meanings. These idioms can be understood literally, and are not difficult to use, which is why most students can easily understand them.

"As free as a bird" is a metaphor that means being as free as a bird. "A dog in the manger" literally refer to a dog in a stable, but in fact it means to occupy a resource without using it, obstructing the development of others. This idiom is often used to describe people who are selfish and greedy. These idioms, whether expressed plainly or through the use of explicit or implicit metaphors, have a certain connection between their literal and actual meanings, making it relatively easy to infer their correct meanings.

All of the above demonstrates the semantic features of English idioms—holism, transparency (decomposability), and specificity. The features of holism and transparency are generally applicable to all idioms. The higher the transparency of an idiom, the easier it is for students to understand. We must comprehend idioms as a whole and not break down their constituent words. Many idioms have a two-sided meaning, and those that involve metaphorical language require careful inferences of their extended meaning, otherwise it is easy to misunderstand and use improperly. Idioms with low transparency require us to understand their evolution or correct meaning, and we should not rely on our subjective guessing. In addition, when understanding and using English idioms, we must pay attention to their specificity and avoid using analogies to deduce unknown meanings or creating new idioms based on known meanings using analogy. Therefore, understanding and grasping the semantic features of idioms is particularly important, and semantic analysis is a necessary strategy for college students to comprehend English idioms.

Table 7-2　The Correct Rate of Each Question

Question	The correct number of people	Accuracy rate
1	34	68%
2	27	54%
3	27	54%

Continued

Question	The correct number of people	Accuracy rate
4	20	40%
5	26	52%
6	8	16%
7	25	50%
8	26	52%
9	21	42%
10	19	38%
11	25	50%
12	27	54%
13	16	32%
14	27	54%
15	18	36%
16	35	70%
17	6	12%
18	37	74%
19	11	22%
20	27	54%
21	28	56%
22	17	34%
23	29	58%
24	29	58%
25	33	66%

2) Interview results and discussion

The researchers interviewed six students, all of whom were very active in their work and answered the questions in the interview honestly. The communication with the students went very smoothly, and the researchers carefully recorded the contents of the interview. The students' responses were as follows:

a. How do you acquire and learn English idioms?

A: I mostly learn them in English class, where the teacher teaches us many English idioms.

B: I usually learn them through English class, and I also read some English newspapers to accumulate some English idioms.

C: Sometimes I learn English idioms online, and other times I listen to English broadcasts or watch English news on TV.

D: I generally learn English idioms in English class, and after class, I read some English novels and classics.

E: I often watch English movies or TV series to increase my vocabulary.

F: I prefer music, besides studying English idioms carefully in class, I listen to a lot of English songs and get to know many English idioms.

b. How do you comprehend English idioms?

A: I usually understand and translate idioms literally, and if there are difficult idioms, I search for their meaning online.

B: First, I make sure I know the meaning of every word in the idiom. If there are unfamiliar words, I look them up in the dictionary and then connect the meanings of each word.

C: I first understand the literal meaning of the words and then understand the true meaning of the idiom based on the context.

D: I analyze the rhetoric and grammar of the idiom, then connect it to the context to determine the meaning of the idiom.

E: I often understand idioms based on their literal meaning. If I don't understand, I will ask the teacher.

F: I guess the meaning of the idiom based on the meaning of the words within the idiom, but often when I look at the correct answer, I realize that my understanding of the idiom's meaning is completely wrong.

c. What problems are you confronted with in comprehending English idioms?

A: I have an insufficient vocabulary and often misunderstand the meaning of English idioms when I encounter unfamiliar words.

B: Often, the meaning of English idioms is completely different from the literal meaning of the words, and I don't know how to grasp the true meaning of the idiom.

C: When I understand English idioms, I do not understand the rhetorical device contained in the idiom, so I often make mistakes.

D: I lack an understanding of the culture of English-speaking countries. I do not understand some of the metaphorical or emotional connotations of English words in idioms, leading to misunderstandings.

E: I often ignore the role of context for understanding English idioms and frequently misunderstand them.

F: I only understand the literal meaning of English idioms and do not know how to deduce their metaphorical or extended meanings.

Through communication with students, we can learn that college students acquire English idioms through various channels, including: (a) in English classes where teachers teach idioms; (b) reading English newspapers, novels, and classics; (c) listening to English songs, broadcasts, or news; and (d) watching English movies or TV shows. Most students rely on literal translation or look up the meaning of idioms in dictionaries, turn to teachers for help, or search online for its correct meaning. Only a minority of students comprehend idioms by analyzing the rhetorical devices used in idioms. There are often many problems for college students in comprehending idioms, such as: (a) lack of vocabulary; (b) not paying attention to analyzing the rhetoric used in idioms or carrying out semantic analysis, leading to literal understanding of idioms; and (c) disregarding the context in which idioms are used.

7.2.4 Conclusion

7.2.4.1 Summary and recommendations

In summary, this study aims to explore the comprehending of English idioms by college students from a semantic perspective. Empirical research has revealed that there are many problems in the comprehending of idioms by college students. Semantic analysis plays a vital role in comprehending idioms, and this study examines effective ways for college students to comprehend idioms. English idioms have their own unique features, which are primarily manifested in their semantic unity and structural fixedness. Idioms are indivisible entities, their meanings possess a holistic nature, and they cannot often be inferred from the literal meanings of their constituent parts. The overall meaning of an idiom often deviates from the literal meanings of its individual components, some being closer in meaning to their literal meaning, while others differ greatly or are completely unrelated. Therefore, semantic analysis should be the primary strategy for English learners to comprehend idioms. This study also makes both teachers and students realize that learning idioms is not about memorizing by rote, but has internal regularities. It provides theoretical and methodological guidance for Chinese college students to comprehend and acquire English idioms, and offers new ways of thinking for teaching English idioms to improve teaching efficiency.

The following are some suggestions for comprehending English idioms from the perspective of semantics:

1) Since idioms have the feature of holism, they must be understood as a whole, avoiding literal interpretations that break the semantic integrity and result in a different meaning from the true meaning.

2) Students should attempt to understand the metaphorical concepts behind idioms, paying attention to the internal connections between the constituent parts and the overall meaning, and deducing the extended meaning in turn. Teachers should also emphasize the metaphorical concepts in their idiom instruction, focusing on developing the students' metaphorical skills.

3) Teachers should attempt to explain the semantic features of idioms and guide college students to quickly and scientifically comprehend and acquire English idioms from a semantic perspective.

4) Students should expand their vocabulary and acquire idioms through diverse ways, enriching their knowledge related to idioms. Only with abundant vocabulary can students minimize errors in the process of acquiring English idioms.

5) Since English idioms have a wide range of sources, students should try to understand their origins. By exploring their sources, one can further understand and grasp the profound meaning of idioms.

7.2.4.2 Limitations of the Study

Due to the lack of time, this study has the following limitations.

First, the number of people participating in questionnaires and interviews, as well as the idioms of the test, is small, so the data collected in the empirical research is not sufficient, which may affect the research results.

Secondly, because the results of questionnaire surveys and interview surveys are affected by the cooperative attitude of the subjects, if they are not clear about the meaning and purpose of some surveys, adopt a perfunctory attitude to answer at will, and do not answer truthfully, then the objectivity of the survey will be affected. The limitations of this study are expected to be supplemented in future studies.

7.3 English Idiom Comprehension From the Pragmatic Perspective

7.3.1 Introduction

From the pragmatic perspective, acquiring pragmatic meaning of idioms is crucial to successful English idiom acquisition. Without understanding the pragmatics of idioms and not using idioms appropriately according to the context, it will lead to communication failure, and even cause great misunderstanding between the two sides of the communication. Idioms have different stylistic colors and different emotional colors, and the context they apply to is different. We need to choose the appropriate idioms according to the context. Chinese students often make pragmatic mistakes in their use of idioms, including linguistic pragmatic errors and social pragmatic errors. Each of these errors has their causes. When students acquire idioms, if they adopt pragmatic analysis methods, they can acquire the pragmatic usage of idioms and avoid pragmatic errors, so that they can acquire idioms in all aspects and use idioms appropriately in appropriate contexts.

7.3.2 Pragmatic Characteristics of Idioms

Idioms are a common usage and special expression in the English language, and are the essence of the language. They are the most commonly used language phenomenon in daily communication. English idioms contain rich cultural and pragmatic meanings, with multiple pragmatic functions in communication activities. In the introduction of the "Collins COBUILD English Idioms Dictionary" (1998), there is a quote that says, "Idioms have important pragmatic functions in language."

In his book "Idioms and Idiomaticity", Fernando has discussed at length how idioms with interpersonal pragmatic features often reflect the speaker's adherence to pragmatic principles, especially politeness principles, to varying degrees in everyday conversations. He states that idioms with interpersonal pragmatic features are markers of being polite or friendly in daily communication. Establishing friendly relationships in communication is an important foundation for obtaining information, and therefore, people must follow the pragmatic principles that should be observed in the communication process. A considerable number of idioms with interpersonal pragmatic features are often used by people as customary expressions to observe pragmatic principles. The following are some examples of English idioms as specific applications of pragmatic principles in communication.

7.3.2.1 The Role of Idioms in Communication That Follow the "Agreement and Praise Criteria" of Pragmatic Principles

According to Stubbs (2000), idioms play three roles in communication following the "agreement criteria" First, to express that the communicators hold the same point of view. Second, to show that the communicators agree with each other's words and that the conversation is continuing. Third, to demonstrate that the communicators accept each other's point of view and that the topic is being established and developed.

Consider the following examples:

1)A: Yes, about half the size of a guinea pig.

B: Yeah.

A: Doesn't have the same teeth arrangement but I'm not exactly sure what the difference is.

B: Ah, thank you very much.

A: A pleasure

B: But it's a Greek animal.

A: Yes, it is indeed. But yes, you are right.

In conversation 1), "thank you very much" expresses "agreement or recognition" of the other person's words, "A pleasure" expresses "acceptance or appreciation" of the other person's words, while "it is indeed" and "you are right" express "praise" for the other person's point of view.

2)A: How does this cost?

B: A good question (looks up price list)

Conversation 2) is a short dialogue between a customer and a shop assistant. "A good question" not only expresses the shop assistant's "praise or recognition" of the customer's words, but also conceals the fact that the shop assistant cannot answer the customer's question at the moment. At the same time, it also plays a role in maintaining and developing the conversation.

7.3.2.2 The Role of Idioms in Communication That Follow the "Appropriateness and Modesty Criteria" of Pragmatic Principles

In order to "save face" for the other person, people in communication need to "minimize the loss to others and maximize the benefit to others" or "minimize their own praise and maximize their own depreciation." The idioms used in the following examples serves the principles of "appropriateness" and "modesty".

1) I'm afraid I don't have a brochure.
2) I'm sorry to say that Terry is unable to be with us.
3) I'm afraid I have to stop you there.

The pragmatic function of idioms is also reflected in language communication activities. English idioms usually express the speaker's attitude, indicate the background of the speech, and reflect the social relationship between the two communicators. They have evaluative, contextual, and cultural identity functions. The application of English idioms enables the communicators to quickly anticipate the intentions or meanings of each other's speech, thus making the entire communication activity smooth, efficient, and effortless. The use of idioms can sometimes even play a key role in establishing, maintaining, or negotiating communication relationships. The characteristics of pragmatics are closely related to our environment, customs, and culture. The following will illustrate the relationship between pragmatical characteristics with environment, customs, and culture.

a. Differences in living environments

The origin of idioms is closely related to people's labor and life. Britain is an island nation, and its maritime industry once led the world in history. On the other hand, the Han nationality lives and reproduces on the Asian continent, and people's lives cannot do without the land. For example, in English, the idiom "spend money like water" means wasting money generously, while in Chinese, the equivalent idiom is "spend money like dirt." There are many idioms in English related to ships and water, which do not have exact counterparts in Chinese, such as "to rest on one's oars" (take a break for the time being), "to keep one's head above water" (strive to survive), and "all at sea" (bewildered). In the cultural atmosphere of Chinese, "dōng fēng" refers to "spring wind," and summer is often associated with scorching heat. "chì rì yán yán sì huǒ shāo" and "jiāo yáng sì huǒ" are frequently used to describe summer in Chinese. On the other hand, Britain is located in the western hemisphere and falls within the temperate zone. It has a maritime climate, with news of spring brought by the west wind. Percy Bysshe Shelley's "Ode to the West Wind" is a celebration of spring. The British summer is a delightful and pleasant season, often associated with the qualities of "lovely", "mild" and "wonderful". In one of his sonnets, Shakespeare compares his lover to a summer's day, saying "Shall I compare thee to a summer's day? / Thou art more lovely and more temperate".

b. Differences in customs

There are many differences in customs between English and Chinese, one of the most typical being their attitudes towards dogs. In Chinese, dogs are considered lowly animals, with many idioms containing negative connotations such as *"Hú péng gǒu dǎng"* *"gǒu jí tiào qiáng"* *"láng xīn gǒu fèi"* *"gǒu tuǐ zi"*, and so on. Although the number of people keeping dogs as pets has greatly increased in recent years, the negative image of dogs remains deeply ingrained in Chinese language and culture. In contrast, dogs are considered man's best friend in Western English-speaking countries. While there are some idioms in English that are derogatory toward dogs due to influences from other languages, the majority of them do not contain negative connotations. In English idioms, dog imagery is often used to describe human behavior, such as "You are a lucky dog" "Every dog has his day" and "Old dog will not learn new tricks". In English, the phrase "sick as a dog" is used to describe someone who is very ill, while "dog-tired" refers to extreme exhaustion. Conversely, cats are highly regarded in Chinese culture and the phrase "greedy cat" is used to describe someone who loves to eat, often with a sense of endearment. In Western culture, cats are used as a metaphor for "deceitful women with hidden agendas".

c. Differences in religious beliefs

Many idioms related to religious beliefs also appear in English and Chinese language. Buddhism has a history of over a thousand years in China, and people believe that the "Buddha" is controlling everything in the world. There are many idioms related to this belief, such as "jìe huā xiàn fó" and "xián shí bù shāo xiāng, lín shí bào fó jiǎo". In many Western countries, especially in the UK and US, people believe in Christianity. Related idioms such as "God helps those who help themselves" and curses like "Go to hell" are common.

d. Historical allusions

Both English and Chinese languages also contain countless idioms that originate from historical allusions. These idioms have simple structures, profound meanings, and often cannot be understood or translated solely based on their literal meanings. For example, "*dōng shī xiào pín*" "*míng luò sūn shān*" "*yè gōng hào lóng*", and so on. In English, allusion idioms are mostly derived from the Bible and Greek and Roman mythology, such as "Achilles'heel" (a fatal weakness), "meet one's Waterloo" (suffer a crushing defeat), "Penelope's web" (an impossible task), and "a Pandora's box" (a source of disaster, trouble, or harm).

In recent years, studies on English idioms have developed in the areas of culture, function, and pragmatics. From a cultural perspective, English idioms are considered as specific social-cultural products, and research focuses on examining their origins and the societal-cultural aspects reflected in them. "Idioms and Idiomaticity", written by Australian linguist Fernando (1996), investigates English idioms in the context of language communication and considers the study of idiomatic function as a dynamic research area. The study of English idiomatic function has triggered research into the various aspects of idioms in communication activities, such as their textual function, discourse analysis, contextual meaning, and pragmatic issues.

In communicative activity, in order for both speakers and listeners to be successful in their communication, they must first have certain beliefs that are mutually shared. This allows the purpose and intent of the dialogue to be mutually understood in the communication process. In other words, in the process of dialogue, both parties must have a common conceptual structure in order for communication to be successful.

Pragmatics is a comprehensive study of various factors related to language use. The pragmatic perspective radiates through language phenomena at any structural aspect, whether it is phonetic, lexical, syntactic, or discourse level. Pragmatics conducts a comprehensive study of all aspects of language usage phenomena from cognitive, social, and cultural perspectives. An English idiom is a habitual and special expression of the English language, and are the essence of English language. They are the most commonly used language phenomena in daily communication. As a reflection of social and cultural aspects, English idioms contain rich cultural and pragmatic significance. In communicative activity, idioms have a directive function for social relationships and cultural identity. The use of idioms enables communicants to quickly anticipate the intent or purpose of the other party in the conversation, making the entire communication activity smooth, efficient and effortless.

As McCarthy (1998) states, it is difficult to imagine the effectiveness and fluency of language communication without these ready-made prefabricated units. In our research, we have found that English idioms have diverse cultural connotations, types, and pragmatic functions. The abundant variety of idioms reflects how people use different types of idioms in different contexts. The rich cultural features of idioms reflect the historical development, geography, politics, economics, religious beliefs, fables, myths, literature, arts and other aspects of the English nation. People's exploration of the cultural origins of idioms is actually a pragmatic process. Idioms in English have multiple pragmatic functions, including indicative, organizational, interpersonal, evaluative, economical, educational, contextual and cultural identification functions. The use of English idioms can play a key role in establishing, maintaining, or negotiating communication relationships. In addition, the relationship between the use of English idioms and the context to some extent reflects the intimacy of interpersonal relationships between communicators.

The study of English idioms should not be limited to traditional structure and meaning analysis. The idioms being used in context, especially their function or meaning, should be the focus of the study. Many studies have shown that learners' pragmatic abilities do not naturally develop along with their grammatical abilities and require targeted teaching and training. Furthermore, the existence of pragmatic differences caused by cultural differences makes foreign language learners prone to cross-cultural pragmatic errors, leading to a breakdown in cross-cultural communication. Therefore, pragmatic ability training has received more and more attention in foreign language teaching, and research exploring pragmatic ability training in foreign language teaching is constantly emerging.

These studies either focus on cultural factors in foreign language teaching or explore the role of formulaic language in the development of pragmatic competence in L2 acquisition. Others empirically investigate the effectiveness of explicit teaching in improving non-native speakers' ability to understand conversational implicatures, while some scholars explore theoretical methods for developing pragmatic competence. These studies provide significant explorations of pragmatic competence and its development, but unfortunately, most of them are limited to foreign language teaching or only discuss the necessity and potential ways of developing pragmatic competence theoretically. There are few empirical studies on how to cultivate pragmatic competence in foreign language teaching.

This study aims to analyze the comprehension and use of English idioms by college students from the perspective of pragmatics through questionnaire survey and interviews. It is intended to help college students understand and master the essence and cognitive rules of English idioms, improve their pragmatic ability, and therefore use English idioms effectively, appropriately and fittingly.

7.3.3 Empirical Study on Comprehension Among College Students

7.3.3.1 Research Purpose

Based on previous research and investigations of idioms, this study explores college students' understanding of English idioms from a pragmatic perspective. Specifically, this study aims to:

1) investigate the current situation of English idiom comprehension among college students;

2) explore English idiom comprehension methods from the perspective of pragmatics;

3) conduct English idiom comprehension practice from a pragmatic perspective

7.3.3.2 Research Objectives and Methods

This study conducted a survey and interviews to investigate the proficiency of English idioms from the perspective of pragmatics among 40 students in Guangxi National Normal University. A random survey method was taken, with a total of 40 questionnaires distributed and collected. In the questionnaires, some English idioms used in daily life are listed, which are selected from textbooks and exercises. Interviews are conducted with 5 randomly selected students, aiming to understand their attitudes and opinions towards idioms. The questionnaires are designed for subjects to translate common idiomatic phrases into Chinese. Students needs to consider contextual factors, culture, and customs, which served as reliable indexes to assess their proficiency in idiomatic expressions from a pragmatic perspective.

7.3.3.3 Research Process

To investigate the proficiency of Chinese college students in English idioms from a pragmatic perspective, this questionnaire survey was targeted at 40 students from Guangxi national normal University.

A total of 40 questionnaires were distributed, all of which were considered valid. The survey was conducted on March 15-16, 2022. After collecting the questionnaires, the results were compiled, analyzed, and discussed (as shown in Table 7-3 and Table 7-4).

Table 7-3 Overall Statistics of the Questionnaire

scores	The Number of subjects	Percentage
≥90	4	10%
≥80	10	25%
≥60	18	45%
≤60	8	20%

Table 7-4 Sub-Item Statistics of the Questionnaire

Question	The number of subjects who score	Accuracy rate
1	27	68%
2	20	50%
3	24	60%
4	20	40%
5	26	65%
6	10	25%
7	15	38%
8	20	40%
9	22	55%
10	19	48%

Continued

Question	The number of subjects who score	Accuracy rate
11	25	63%
12	13	33%
13	16	40%
14	20	50%
15	10	25%
16	18	45%
17	22	55%
18	23	58%
19	27	68%
20	16	40%
21	28	70%
22	14	35%
23	20	50%
24	24	60%
25	18	45%

From Table 7-3 and Table 7-4, it can be seen that only 4 students scored above 90 points, with 10 students scoring between 80 and 90 points. Overall, there were 18 students scoring between 60 to 80 points (inclusive of 60 points) and 8 students scoring below 60 points, indicating that the percentage of excellent and failing students was 10% and 20%, respectively.

The following questions are interviewed:
1) How do you usually learn English idioms?
2) What is your attitude towards English idioms?
3) Do you often use English idioms in daily life?

The results are as follows:

1) Among the interviewed students, their methods of learning English idioms include reading books, learning in the classroom, and watching movies in English.

2) Interviewed students generally have a positive attitude towards English idioms, believing that they are an important part of the English language and mastering them is helpful for learning English.

3) English idioms are rarely used in daily life.

These data show that the proficiency of English idioms among college students is low, with limited use of idioms in daily life. There is an urgent need for students to find effective ways to improve their skills in using idiomatic expressions in English.

7.3.3.4 Results and Discussion

1) Results

According to the analysis of the survey among students, the current situation of English idiom comprehension among college students still needs improvement. The research results showed that among the 40 students, there are 10% scored 90 or above, indicating an excellent understanding and grasp of idioms. 25% of the students scored 80 or above, indicating a good understanding and mastery of idioms. 45% of the students scored 60 or above, showing a so-so understanding and mastery of idioms. Additionally, 20% of the students scored below 60, indicating an unsatisfactory result.

2) Discussion

The study presents the current situation of understanding and usage of English idioms among college students in China. It is concluded that there is still room for improvement, as idioms play a special and important role in the English language. Specifically, idioms are commonly used in language communication. For Chinese college students, mastering English not only means having accurate pronunciation, grammar, and sufficient vocabulary, but also involves understanding or mastering a certain number of idioms that reflect the characteristics of the English language. Therefore, to improve students' idiom comprehension, teachers should first raise students' awareness of idioms and help them understand and master the essence and cognitive rules of English idioms. This will enable them to use idioms effectively, appropriately, and appropriately as well as improve their pragmatic language skills in language learning.

7.3.4 Summary

This study explores English idiom comprehension among college students from a pragmatic perspective, using questionnaires and interviews as research methods. Through analysis of the results, it has been found that currently, a part of college students' English idiom comprehension is poor. It is hoped that this study can arouse the attention of teachers and students to the pragmatics of English idioms, and make them realize the importance of idioms. Based on the research findings, some suggestions and methods for acquiring idioms from a pragmatic perspective are proposed:

1) Teachers should introduce more idioms into the classroom, encouraging students to use idioms in their learning and daily life.

2) Teachers can organize competitions related to pragmatic aspects

of idioms to enrich students' knowledge of idioms.

3) Students can learn English idioms by reading English classics or watching English films and TV dramas.

Since the study targeted 40 college students in Guangxi National Normal University, the study has certain limitations and the conclusions drawn may not represent English idiom acquisition among college students nationwide. However, it reveals the situation of some college students' English idiom comprehension and can provide some reference for future research.

7.4 English Idiom Comprehension From the Cultural Perspective

7.4.1 Introduction

If we want to learn the English language well, we need to master the knowledge of cultural background and the ability to analyze cultural context. In the college curriculum, there are also a large number of idioms. Some idioms may seem like simple words and phrases, but they are very difficult to understand. In order to better achieve the teaching goal, let students have a deeper understanding of idioms and grasp knowledge better, it is undoubtedly necessary to study the background and cultural knowledge of idioms in college textbooks. Therefore, this book studies the understanding of English idioms for college students from a cultural perspective.

Some English scholars have made a relatively systematic cultural context analysis of English idioms, studied the unique cultural background of English idioms, cultural origins and differences in cultural context, and the understanding of English idioms. Most of the previous studies covered a wide range of studies, involving college students or English scholars, but there were few specialized and detailed studies of English idioms at the college level. In college textbooks, there are also a large number of idioms. In order to better achieve the teaching purpose, it is undoubtedly necessary to study the background and cultural knowledge of the idioms in college textbooks. This book sorts out the additional cultural information of some idioms in college textbooks, adopts the methods of pre-test and post-test to study the understanding and acquisition of English idioms of college students from the perspective of culture, and specifically analyzes the use of idioms in different contexts, so that college students can better understand and achieve the teaching purpose of teachers.

7.4.2 Understanding English Idioms in a Cultural Context

Cultural context was first proposed in anthropologist Malinowski's interpretation of the concept of "context". Context can be divided into situational context and cultural context. Cultural context refers to the sociocultural context in which language is embedded for communicative purposes. It generally encompasses two aspects: cultural customs, which refer to the inherited and customary patterns of life of the people in social interactions, representing the collective habits of a social group in terms of language, behavior, and psychology, with normative and constraining effects on the members belonging to that group; and social norms, which refer to the various regulations and restrictions imposed by a society on verbal communicative activities. English idioms are closely tied to the culture of a country or a nation.

7.4.2.1 Idioms and Historical Development

The development of social history has a tremendous impact on language. For instance, wars, conquests, and significant historical events can give rise to new idioms, introduce foreign words, and even assign new meanings to existing words. Take the word "jeep" as an example. During World War II, American soldiers were avid readers of the comic strip "Popeye," which featured an interesting creature named Jeep. The pronunciation of "jeep" was similar to the military vehicle at that time (General Jeep, G.P), leading to the term "jeep" being used for the vehicle we know today. However, as time passes and circumstances change, we cannot turn back time, but we can find traces of history in idioms.

Major historical events have also left behind numerous idioms for future generations. For example, the Roman conquest has given rise to many idioms related to Rome, such as "Rome was not built in a day" (referring to the notion that great achievements require time) and "Do in Rome as the Romans do" (referring to the idea of adapting to local customs). Some customs from that era have been passed down through idioms as well. For instance, the expression "bear the palm" is now used to describe victory because in ancient Rome, victorious fighters were crowned with palm branches or wreaths made of palm leaves as symbols of victory.

The idiom "rain cats and dogs" is used to describe heavy rain. In Norse mythology, Odin, the chief god of the ancient Norsemen, is associated with wind (represented by dogs) and rain (represented by cats), hence "It is raining cats and dogs" meaning a heavy downpour. The phrase "pan out" is now used to mean success. In 1848, a man discovered gold in California. The news quickly spread, and people flocked to the area, sparking the gold rush. People used pans to sift through sand in streams to extract gold, hence the term "pan out."

From the Roman conquest to the conquests of the Teutonic people, and to the Norman conquest, the independence of the North American colonies, and the World War II period, rich idioms have been left behind in every era. It would be quite challenging to list them all. To become proficient in these idioms, one must study the historical events behind them. Only by understanding their origins and contexts can one fully grasp and learn them.

7.4.2.2 Idioms and the Natural Environment

The formation of culture is inseparable from a specific natural geographic environment. People living in different geographic environments naturally develop different cultures. Since ancient times, there has been an intimate relationship between humans and nature. The natural environment provides conditions for human beings, such as fishing in the sea and grazing in the wilderness. All of this is closely related to the natural environment. Through idioms, we can learn how our ancestors hunted, fished, cultivated, and their reverence and love for nature.

In the UK, with its dense river networks, winding coastlines, and numerous islands that are easily navigable, there have emerged numerous idioms related to fishing and navigation. For example, "All at sea" is now used to mean being confused or disoriented, but it used to refer to a ship losing control and drifting with the wind, with people on board not knowing their whereabouts. For example, "She is all at sea as to what to do next."

"Raise the wind" refers to the fact that sailing relies on wind, especially during the era of sailing ships. Hence, the term emerged to metaphorically mean "raising money." For example, "We decided to buy a house, and father said he'd raise the wind somehow."

"See how the land lies" means understanding the topography, and "see how the wind blows" means detecting the wind direction. In sailing, understanding the topography and wind direction is crucial to determine the course and sailing time. Nowadays, both idioms mean "observing the situation and understanding the circumstances." For example, "We must see how the land lies before we decide whether to start our plan."

Fishing plays a significant role in the UK's economy, and as a result, there are numerous idioms related to fishing. "Like a fish out of water" describes feeling uncomfortable or out of place in an unfamiliar environment. For example, "She felt like a fish out of water at a new school." "Drink like a fish" is an idiom that metaphorically means drinking alcohol excessively, rather than drinking water like a fish. For example, "The man drinks like a fish." "Make fish of one and flesh of another" means showing favoritism or treating individuals differently. For example, "The two children quickly realized that their parents make fish of one and flesh of another."

Livestock farming and poultry breeding are well-developed in the UK. Livestock farming accounts for 70% of the total agricultural output value and has left behind many related idioms. "All wool and a yard wide" refers to the finest wool when all the wool is a yard long. It metaphorically means a person who is generous and kind-hearted. For example, "She's a grateful mother—all wool and a yard wide." "Wool-gathering" originally referred to gathering scattered wool from fences by shepherds to avoid waste. It is now used metaphorically to describe being absent-minded or inattentive during work. For example, "I am tired of my constant wool-gathering during my work."

"Much cry and little wool" means making a lot of noise but producing little result. It is now used to describe a situation where there is much talk but little action. For example, "Her diary was much more cry than wool."

Great Britain is located in the temperate maritime climate zone in the western part of the European continent. It experiences abundant rainfall, strong winds, and fog throughout the year. Therefore, rain is a common occurrence for the British. "As right as rain" means that rain is normal, and the absence of rain would be considered unusual. Due to rain being a common occurrence, when people make appointments to do something, they often add "come rain or shine" at the end, meaning that they will come regardless of whether it rains or the weather is fine. However, there are still occasions when events are canceled due to rain, which is referred to as being "rained off." For example, "The match was rained off."

7.4.2.3 Idioms and Customs

Customs and traditions are created by social groups and are not products of individual factors. The way of life of people in a particular region is their customs and traditions, which encompass a wide range of things, including politics, economy, culture, religion, literature, and art. They influence and interact with each other. The language of a nation inevitably reflects its customs and traditions, and idioms are closely related to the customs and traditions of a nation.

The geographic environment in which people reside has a significant impact on their dietary habits. In the regions where various European ethnic groups live, the main grain crops are wheat, barley, and oats. Wheat is used to bake bread, barley is used for brewing beer, and oats are used to feed livestock. Bread is not only the staple food of the British but has also been brought to various parts of the world, especially English-speaking countries in North America and Oceania, by early British immigrants. Bread, butter, jam, and cheese are everyday food for the British, leading to the creation of numerous idioms related to them.

"Earn one's bread" is now used to mean "earn a living". For example, "She earns her bread by working in a factory." The idiom "bread and butter" has multiple figurative meanings because bread and butter are staple foods for Westerners, with a long history in English-speaking countries. The following are some of its main meanings:

(1) Basic, practical, every day. For example, "It is a real bread-and-butter satellite."

(2) Expressing thanks for the hospitality received. For example, "The guest gave a usual bread-and-butter letter to the host."

(3) Ordinary and mundane. For example, "The students asked some bread-and-butter questions."

(4) Childish, student-like. For example, "She is still a bread-and-butter miss."

"Butter up" metaphorically means "flatter" or "please excessively." For example, "He began to butter up the superior in hope of being given a better job."

Around the early 17th century, tea from China was introduced to Britain. Despite being expensive at the time, it was warmly welcomed by the British and quickly became popular. Tea became a traditional and popular beverage for the British, leading to the creation of many idioms related to tea.

"For all the tea in China" refers to the high value of all the tea in China. However, this idiom is often used in the negative sense, meaning that one would not do something no matter how high the reward or offer is. For example, "The environment in that company is too bad, I wouldn't go back to that job for all the tea in China."

In addition to being essential in people's lives, pets have gradually formed a "pet culture" and occupy an important place in people's lives. Every nation has its favorite animals, and the British have a particular fondness for dogs, resulting in many idioms related to dogs, such as "lucky dog" "yellow dog" and "big dog". The idiom "Keep a dog and bark oneself" metaphorically means doing the work oneself even though there are others to do it or doing the work of subordinates. For example, "I would not do the housework if my wife is at home; that would be keeping a dog and barking myself." The idiom "Love me, love my dog" means that anyone who wants to maintain friendship with me must accept and tolerate everything that belongs to me, similar to the concept of loving both the person and their possessions. Having a good name can often be easily remembered by others, so choosing a good name is highly important. In English, personal names often appear in idioms. Personal names in idioms generally fall into two categories: those derived from historical events and become idioms through long-term usage, and those derived from customs, folklore, or commonly used names. For example, "every man jack" means "everyone" or "every person". For example, "We lived on the earth, too, every man Jack of us".

7.4.2.4 Idioms and Religious Beliefs

Religion is an important part of human thought and culture, originating even in primitive societies. Different religions reflect different cultural characteristics and backgrounds. Religion is a cultural phenomenon, and idioms are closely related to culture. Many idioms in English are closely associated with religion. For example, "go to the church" played a significant role in feudal society, where Christianity was prominent. The Bible, as a classic representation of Christian theology, has widely circulated and contains many stories, from which numerous idioms originate.

"At the eleventh hour" comes from a story in the New Testament of the Bible, specifically in the Gospel of Matthew, chapter 20. It is now used to describe doing something at the last moment. For example, "I arrived at the classroom at the eleventh hour."

"The apple of one's eye" originates from Psalm 17:8 in the Old Testament of the Bible, which expresses the desire to be kept as the apple of God's eye. It is now used to describe someone who is cherished and highly valued. For example, "The little girl was the apple of her parents' eye."

"Old Adam" comes from chapters 2 and 3 of the book of Genesis in the Old Testament. Adam is seen as representing the sinful nature of humanity. It is now used to describe the inherent evil nature of a person. For example, "People's real enemy is the Old Adam."

7.4.3 Empirical study on English Idiom Comprehension Among College Students

7.4.3.1 Purpose and Significance of the Study

For English language learners, idioms present a significant challenge. During the busy stage of college, students often neglect the study of idioms, overlook their cultural context, and believe that it's enough to memorize words and understand grammar. However, for most people, even if they know the meaning of each word in an English idiom, they often find it hard to understand the overall meaning; even if they understand its literal meaning, it's usually difficult to infer its metaphorical and extended meanings, and even harder to use it properly.

In the college curriculum, most college teachers can't fully understand the cultural background of idioms, let alone teach it to their students. Most teachers gloss over idioms in class, even asking students to rote learn them. But in daily life, students often encounter many idioms, some of which are difficult to guess, let alone use. To help students better understand idioms and better grasp English knowledge, it's very important to strengthen the explanation of the cultural background of idioms in classroom teaching.

7.4.3.2 Research Methods and Processes

In order to verify the necessity of explaining the cultural background of idioms in teaching, the author surveyed some non-English majors at Guangxi national normal University in China. The class has a total of 30 students, and the average score of English in the final exam in July ranks in the middle of the grade. It was found that these students had never learned about the cultural background of idioms in their English learning.

The method of pre-test and post-test is adopted for this research. Considering the current situation of the students' knowledge of English idioms, the test questions are in the form of multiple-choice questions. There are three steps in this research. The first step is to distribute questionnaires to the students for a pre-test on their understanding of English idioms. The pre-test questionnaire consists of 30 multiple-choice questions on idioms, each worth five points for a total of 150 points, with three options set for each question. The 30 questions are idioms related to biblical stories, sports and entertainment, natural environment, animals, plants, economy, body parts, politics, classic literature, myths and fable stories, with three idioms for each category. The questions are comparable to the level of college students. The second step is to intersperse the cultural background knowledge of some idioms in classroom teaching, guiding students to understand and use some relevant idioms. The teaching lasts for three months, with each class allocating approximately 10 to 15 minutes to explain English idioms. The idioms are roughly categorized in the explanation, so as to instill an awareness of them in the students.

Firstly, it's important to understand what idioms are, and to learn about their definition. Following this, the idioms are categorized into various groups, including biblical stories, sports and entertainment, natural environment, animals, plants, economy, body parts, politics, classic literature, myths and fable stories. Each category varies, and teachers can decide according to the situation. Next, some idioms from the university stage are selected for in-depth explanation. This includes discussing their literal meanings, metaphorical meanings, and the additional cultural information behind them. Finally, practice and application are emphasized. Students are encouraged to practice and use the idioms they have learned, such as making sentences, practicing dialogues, and making educated guesses about idioms they have not learned before.

The third step involves a post-test to evaluate students' understanding of English idioms. The post-test questionnaire contains a total of 30 multiple-choice questions on idioms, each question has three options, each question is worth five points, adding up to a total of 150 points. The 30 questions are idioms related to biblical stories, sports and entertainment, natural environment, animals, plants, economy, body parts, politics, classic literature, myths and fable stories, with three idioms for each category. The idioms' difficulty level is comparable to that of the pre-test. After three months of study, whether the students' understanding of English idioms has changed is examined.

7.4.3.3 Results and Discussion

1) Results

After conducting the pre-test, according to the statistics, the class average score was 72 points. After the post-test, the class average score was 91 points. Overall, the scores have significantly improved, which shows that paying attention to the explanation of cultural background knowledge of idioms in the teaching process has a certain effect. Although the overall score is not outstanding, the students' awareness of the cultural background knowledge of idioms has significantly improved.

2) Discussion

In the pre-test, the accuracy rate for each question is shown in Table 7-5.

Table 7-5 The Accuracy Rate for Each Question in the Pre-Test

Questions	Options		
	A	B	C
1. At the eleventh hour	73.33%	20%	6.67%
2. last supper	6.67%	93.33%	0%
3. Judas kiss	73.33%	26.67%	0%
4. go for it	73.33%	26.67%	0%
5. in the long run	40%	53.33%	6.67%
6. fly a kite	50%	43.33%	6.67%
7. put an ear to the ground	3.33%	93.33%	3.33%
8. in all weathers	20%	80%	0%
9. in hot water	80%	13.33%	6.67%

Continued

Questions	Options		
	A	B	C
10. a dark horse	53.33%	46.67%	0%
11. love me love my dog	36.67	60%	3.33%
12. as cute as a bug	43.33%	40%	16.67%
13. bed of roses	30%	53.33%	16.67%
14. a hot potato	33.33%	46.67%	20%
15. gild the lily	50%	46.67%	3.33%
16. like a house on fire	26.67%	66.67%	6.67%
17. bottom line	63.33%	36.67%	0%
18. make there	30%	56.67%	13.33%
19. break a leg	46.67%	46.67%	6.67%
20. all thumbs.	53.33%	36.67%	10%
21. Be all ears	43.33%	50%	6.67%
22. loose cannon	46.67%	33.33%	20%
23. top gun	13.33%	80%	6.67%
24. baby kisser	46.67%	46.67%	6.67%
25. hit the mark	66.67%	23.33%	10%
26. jam tomorrow	16.67%	66.67%	16.67%
27. a sorry sight	70%	30%	0%
28. pandora's box	43.33%	53.33%	3.33%
29. a dog in the manger	40%	56.67%	3.33%
30. Lion's Share	63.33%	30%	6.67%

In the test, Questions 1, 2, and 3 were related to biblical stories, with accuracy rates of 73.33%, 93.33%, and 73.33%, respectively, with an average of 79.99%. Questions 4, 5, and 6 were related to sports and entertainment, with accuracy rates of 73.33%, 6.67%, and 43.33%, respectively, with an average of 41.11%. Questions 7, 8, and 9 were related to the natural environment, with accuracy rates of 93.33%, 80%, and 80%, respectively, with an average of 84.44%. Questions 10, 11, and 12 were related to animals, with accuracy rates of 46.67%, 60%, and 40%, respectively, with an average of 48.89%. Questions 13, 14, and 15 were related to plants, with accuracy rates of 53.33%, 20% and 46.67% respectively, averaging 40%. Questions 16, 17, and 18 were related to economics, with accuracy rates of 66.67%, 63.33% and 56.67% respectively, averaging 62.22%. Questions 19, 20, and 21 were related to human body parts, with accuracy rates of 6.67%, 53.33% and 50% respectively, averaging 36.67%. Questions 22, 23 and 24 were related to politics, with accuracy rates of 20%, 80% and 6.67% respectively, averaging 35.56%. Questions 25, 26, and 27 were related to classic literature, with accuracy rates of 66.67%, 66.67% and 0% respectively, averaging 44.45%. Questions 28, 29 and 30 were related to mythology and fable stories, with accuracy rates of 53.33%, 40% and 63.33% respectively, averaging 52.22%.

The results of the pre-test show the following:

1) Students scored higher on some familiar idioms, such as "last supper" which had a score rate of 93.33%.

2) Students scored lower on idioms related to politics, animals, and plants.

3) Students' understanding of idioms is still limited to their literal meanings, neglecting their cultural background knowledge.

After three months of teaching, the accuracy rate of the post-test answers is shown in Table 7-6.

Table 7-6 The Accuracy Rate of Each Question in the Post-Test

Questions	Options		
	A	B	C
1. Adam's Apple	60%	33.33%	6.67%
2. clean hands	33.33%	43.33%	23.33%
3. Judas kiss	93.33%	6.67%	0
4. go for it	6.67%	83.33%	10%
5. jump the gun	40%	56.67%	3.33%
6. pull one's weight	20%	53.33	26.67%
7. break the ice	20%	70%	10%
8. Blood is thicker than water	10%	73.33%	16.67%
9. in the wind	23.23%	76.67%	0%
10. a little bird told me	40%	60%	0%
11. fish in troubled waters	93.33%	6.67%	0%
12. the black sheep	33.33%	23.33%	43.33%
13. couch potato	83.33%	3.33%	13.33%
14. sour grapes	13.33%	80%	6.67%
15. beat around the bush	26.67%	70%	3.33%
16. worth one's salt	30%	63.33%	6.67%
17. strike it rich	80%	10%	10%
18. get the sack	13.33%	76.67%	10%

Continued

Questions	Options		
	A	B	C
19. pay through the nose	13.33%	83.33%	3.33%
20. wet behind the ears	23.33%	67.67%	10%
21. bite your tongue	56.67%	40%	3.33%
22. dry run	16.67%	63.33%	20%
23. field day	80%	10%	10%
24. hot seat	50%	40%	10%
25. as pure as the driven snow	80%	16.67%	3.33%
26. bag and baggage	50%	40%	10%
27. heart's content	66.67%	30%	3.33%
28. Helen of Troy	36.67%	56.67%	6.67%
29. swan song	93.33%	6.67%	0%
30. under the Rose	23.33%	73.33%	3.33%

In the post-test, Questions 1, 2, and 3 were related to biblical stories, with accuracy rates of 60%, 23.33%, and 93.33% respectively, averaging 58.89%, a decrease of 21.1% compared to the pre-test. Questions 4, 5, and 6 were related to sports and entertainment, with accuracy rates of 83.33%, 40% and 26.67% respectively, averaging 50%, an increase of 8.89% compared to the pre-test. Questions 7, 8 and 9 were related to natural environment, with accuracy rates of 70%, 16.67% and 76.67%, averaging 54.45%, a decrease of 29.99% compared to the pre-test. Questions 10, 11 and 12 were related to animals, with accuracy rates of 76.67%, 60% and 96.67% respectively, averaging 77.78%, an increase of 28.89% compared to the pre-test. Questions 13, 14 and 15 were related to the plants, with accuracy rates of 83.33%, 80% and 70% respectively, averaging 77.78%, an increase of 37.78% compared to the pre-test. Questions 16, 17 and 18 were related to economics, with accuracy rates of 63.33%, 80% and 76.67% respectively, averaging 73.33%, an increase of 11.11% compared to the pre-test. Questions 19, 20 and 21 were related to human body parts, with accuracy rates of 3.33%, 67.67% and 56.67% respectively, averaging 42.56%, an increase of 5.89% compared to the pre-test. Questions 22, 23 and 24 were related to politics, with accuracy rates of 20%, 80% and 10% respectively, averaging 36.67%, an increase of 1.11% compared to the pre-test. Questions 25, 26 and 27 were related to classic literary works, with accuracy rates of 80%, 50% and 66.67% respectively, averaging 65.56%, an increase of 21.11% compared to the pre-test. Questions 28, 29 and 30 were related to mythology and fable stories, with accuracy rates of 36.67%, 93.33% and 73.33% respectively, averaging 67.78%, an increase of 15.56% compared with the pre-test.

The results of the pre-test show the following:

1) The overall accuracy of the answers has improved, but the scores are still not high.

2) The scores for idioms related to politics and economics have improved, but the score rate is still not high. There is an improvement on idioms related to animals and plants.

3) Students no longer simply choose the literal meaning of idioms but have developed some awareness of the cultural background knowledge behind idioms. The experimental results indicate that incorporating cultural background knowledge of idioms into college

classroom teaching is conducive to students' comprehending English idioms.

7.4.4 Summary

Understanding English idioms is undoubtedly difficult for college students. In the process of learning English, we will encounter a lot of English idioms. We not only need to know the meaning of idioms but also need to understand the cultural background knowledge behind them. Based on previous research, this article adopts a pre-test and post-test method from a cultural perspective to study the understanding and acquisition of English idioms by college students. The results show that teaching students English idioms from a cultural perspective in the classroom can promote their learning. If students want to improve their knowledge of English idioms, they must pay attention to the cultural knowledge behind the idioms while constantly learning and accumulating English idioms.

8 English Idiom Acquisition Strategies

The new college English teaching syllabus not only sets higher requirements for students' language knowledge and language skills, but also aims to improve students' overall literacy by focusing on emotional attitudes, learning strategies, and cultural awareness. Researching strategies for college students to acquire English idioms not only seeks the best methods for this particular group, but also explores the best shortcut for Chinese students to learn English effectively.

This chapter mainly studies the strategy of idiom acquisition among college students. Starting from the current situation of English learning in Chinese universities, this chapter seeks to explore students' comprehending and acquiring of idioms from social factors, school education, and personal factors, and proposes relevant strategies for English idiom acquisition to find the best shortcut for Chinese college students to acquire English idioms and improve their English proficiency.

8.1 Current Situation of College Students' Acquisition of English Idioms

8.1.1 What English Learning Means to College Students in China

College students can be regarded as the future of the country, and they must be well-prepared in many aspects in order to cope with the ever-changing society. Firstly, English has become a major subject in high school and college. Secondly, English is one of the major international languages in today's world and is the most widely used language. According to statistics from 2016, nearly 400 million people speak English as their mother tongue in the world, roughly one in every ten people speaks English. People in countries such as the UK, US, Canada, Australia, and New Zealand all speak English. Additionally, approximately 20 countries use English as an official or second language, with a total of about 800 million people. In other words, almost one in every five people in the world understands English to some extent. If we add the number of English learners in primary and secondary schools around the world, the number of people who can understand English is even greater. English has become the official language of dozens of countries worldwide, and these countries account for over 70% of the world's wealth. Not understanding English means missing out on 70% of opportunities. There is also a large number of non-English speaking countries, such as Japan and the Republic of Korea, which have rapidly integrated into the international market as their economies take flight and English has become popularized, significantly changing the language landscape of these countries. Surveys show that in these countries, the level of English proficiency is positively correlated to personal social status.

  In short, English is an important communication tool in the fields of international politics, military, economy, science and technology, culture, trade, and transportation. With China's continued opening-up, advances in science and technology, and the constant improvement of international status, there is an urgent need to cultivate a large number of foreign language professionals to accelerate China's "Four Modernizations" process and enable our country to play a greater and more active role in international affairs. Therefore, learning English has important practical and far-reaching historical significance in achieving the above goals.

8.1.2 The Current English Teaching Mode of Schools in China

China is a civilization with a long history, and teachers in China are also trained with traditional education. While English is an international language and our learning should be internationalized, we are often limited by various factors. Traditional education mainly involves teachers teaching students to follow along, with limited opportunities for hands-on practice. In English teaching, teachers typically first teach the new words and then analyze the grammar, translate the text and maybe read the text once more. This approach is not conducive to language learning. Language is a spoken form and language learners must practice speaking more and use the language often.

As summarized by Du Yongli (2008), teachers should consciously cultivate students' contextual response and reconstruction ability with specific listening materials. The following measures could be taken:

1) Explaining new words and discussing before listening. Explaining new words and discussing the topic before listening can familiarize students with the material and reduce anxiety.

2) Cultivating logical thinking skills. Analyzing written materials and predicting possible questions to be involved in listening materials would help build students' logical thinking skills.

3) Identifying key words. Key words can help listeners confirm the main content of the listening material and develop contextual inference skills.

4) Introducing social and cultural knowledge. Given that social and cultural knowledge accounts for a growing proportion of listening tests, familiar topics often seem easier. As a result, teachers should guide students to constantly expand their knowledge and enhance their

world knowledge. Teachers should also provide metalanguage information, design communicative tasks, and promote students' oral pragmatics. For example,

1) Providing language material samples. Real or simulated language materials such as movie scripts and spoken language recordings can provide language samples to students, and language materials that contain a particular speech act (such as requests or refutations) can serve as specific examples for learning speech acts.

2) Analyzing and explaining the background of language materials. Analyzing background information such as characters, occasions, and topics involved in language materials can help students compare and analyze the pragmatic meaning of language used in different materials.

3) Observing language materials.

Therefore, in teaching, teachers should make full use of multimedia visual teaching methods to provide students with more natural and real language scenes, guide students to observe and analyze posture, facial expressions, and actions of English and American people, create opportunities for Chinese students to communicate and learn with foreigners, help students develop cultural difference awareness and sensitivity, and improve their pragmatic ability, thereby enhancing their intercultural communication skills.

8.1.3 The Achievements of Chinese College Students in Learning English

English is a major subject in my college, and the methods to test students' achievements are nothing more than tests, exercises, and exams. The goal of learning a language is to achieve balanced development in listening, speaking, reading, writing and translation.

However, due to the current constraints of China's education system, college education still focuses mainly on test-taking and further education entrance exams, which is an aspect that schools, parents, and society all place great emphasis on. Therefore, we can imagine that college students must have strong test-taking abilities and writing skills, and generally have good reading skills. Nevertheless, since their daily studies mainly revolve around preparing for exams, they have little time to practice their oral English and translation skills. Consequently, the current level of English speaking and translation abilities among college students in China is relatively weak, especially those college students from underdeveloped urban and rural areas where teacher and hardware facilities are in need of improvement.

8.1.4 English Learning and English Idiom Acquisition

Idioms are the essence of language and culture. Behind a simple idiom lies extraordinary meaning. Idioms are not artificially created, but intimately related to local cultural customs, linguistic environment, religious beliefs, and so on. To master the English language, considerable knowledge of English idioms and their culture is necessary. As the curriculum reform deepens, learning English is no longer simply learning a few words or phrases. English textbooks contain a lot of information about British and American culture, and students inevitably encounter many idioms when learning. This requires teachers and students to pay attention to the learning of idioms. However, learning idioms is not a simple task, and many idioms require learners to spend a lot of time searching for information and memorizing. For college students, their English learning usually only focuses on how to get high scores in exams, without spending more time on English idiom acquisition. To comprehensively improve the English proficiency of college students, it is necessary to attach importance to the acquisition of English idioms.

8.2 Factors Affecting College Students' Acquisition of English Idioms

Everything has a cause-and-effect relationship, and there are certainly factors that affect college students' learning of English idioms. These factors include personal abilities, language proficiency, and interest in learning the language, as well as external factors such as the influence of the Chinese language environment, school learning environment, teacher's teaching level, and teaching methods.

Research by Xie Hua (2007) shows that there is a positive correlation between familiarity with a language and understanding of idioms. However, the transparency of a language does not seem to have a significant impact on idiom comprehension, and the relationship between the two is not clear. However, the more familiar and transparent the language, the more accurately learners can understand the meaning of idioms. Contextual information can also help English learners understand the literal and figurative meanings of idioms correctly. There is a clear interactive effect between language familiarity and contextual factors. Zhang Lei and Yu Liming (2011) found that there is a significant positive correlation between the inadequate understanding of Chinese and English idiomatic expressions among English language learners and their guessed comprehension and transfer of idiomatic meanings, which has a more important impact than their actual language proficiency. Learners of different English proficiency levels do not have the same perception distance for English idioms, and those with lower English proficiency tend to rely more on their perception of similarities and native language transfer in understanding

English idioms. Yu Jue (2011) shows that there is a significant positive correlation between idiom productive knowledge and English proficiency, with a significant increase in idiom productive knowledge as English proficiency improves. The correlation between idiom spelling knowledge and English proficiency is the highest, and idiom spelling knowledge grows faster than semantic and synonym knowledge. There are significant differences in the three types of idiom productive knowledge among different levels of English proficiency, with interpersonal idioms having the highest productivity, followed by relational idioms, and conceptual idioms having the lowest. Conceptual idioms have the greatest impact on English proficiency and can predict English proficiency. The aforementioned research findings are based on students' own judgments. In teaching activities, teaching and learning are mutual, and teachers play a crucial role in guiding students' learning. Teachers' teaching proficiency and methods constantly influence students' development.

In addition, native language also influences second language acquisition. As a foreign language, English learning is inevitably affected by language environment, social environment, language differences, and students' desire to learn English. First, Chinese as a native language affects English pronunciation. English is spelled with words, while Chinese is spelled with pinyin and then expressed with characters. Secondly, Chinese grammar affects English grammar. Chinese sentence structure and logic are different from English, especially in idioms. Furthermore, fixed Chinese thinking and expression have an impact on the acquisition of English idioms, and Chinese-style English may occur when understanding idioms. Taking the response to praise as an example, Yuan and Li (2011) investigated the Chinese pragmatic ability of American Chinese and non-Chinese students. The results showed that second language pragmatic ability can be formed and developed in the classroom, and there is an important relationship between the acquisition of second language pragmatic ability, learning motivation, identity recognition and mother tongue pragmatic habits. This fully illustrates the impact of mother tongue and mother tongue environment on learning a second language. Therefore, some strategies will be proposed below to provide better methods for college students to master English idioms.

8.3 English Idiom Acquisition Strategies for College Students in China

8.3.1 Strategy of Preparation

Teachers play a leading role in the teaching process, and the level of students' English proficiency is directly related to the teacher's teaching methods. Therefore, it is necessary to improve the teacher's teaching level in idioms and change their teaching methods. During the process of learning English, teachers and learners will definitely encounter many idioms. Teachers should attach importance to the teaching of English idioms. Allowing teachers to lead students to learn idioms is more conducive to students' acquisition of idioms. For example, teachers should list out idioms separately when preparing for class, and for cultural background idioms, teachers should find information in advance to explain to students in class; or teachers can assign tasks for students to find the origin of idioms after class, so as to gradually attract students' attention and cultivate their interest in learning idioms.

8.3.2 Strategy of Guessing Based on Context

When encountering an idiom during reading, teachers can ask students to guess the meaning of the idiom based on the context of the context. By giving the initiative to the students and mobilizing their enthusiasm, they can actively use their imagination or inference ability. Only when they cannot guess the meaning of an idiom correctly, should the teacher provide guidance.

8.3.3 Inductive Strategy

According to the requirements of the teaching syllabus and the content of the text, teachers guide students to classify and summarize idioms. All the idioms encountered in the learning process should be classified according to a certain classification method, such as classifying them by theme, sorting idioms related to Greek mythology, Aesop's Fables, Bible stories, animals, plants, economics, politics, classic literary works, and so on, and then memorize them.

8.3.4 Repetitive Practice Strategy

Idioms are generally conventional, and they have their unique characteristics. For second language learners, to learn idioms well in a Chinese-language environment, the key is to have a lot of exposure to and practice with idioms. Learners need to practice it repeatedly, and often use idioms for communication or writing.

8.3.5 Strategy of Using Idiomatic Knowledge in the Mother Tongue

When encountering idioms, learners can first learn to use the knowledge of idioms in their mother tongue to deduce the meaning of English idioms based on their literal meaning. If this does not work, then they can use other strategies to learn idioms.

English idioms are the essence of language, and learning English idioms is not an easy task. College students who want to better grasp

English idioms need to adjust their attitudes, motivate their enthusiasm for learning, and try to get rid of the influence of their Chinese mother tongue environment. At the same time, they should attach importance to the teacher's guidance and education. Teachers should take the lead, change their teaching methods, actively guide students to learn English idioms, and work hard to enable students to better grasp English idioms.

9 Model Construction of English Idiom Acquisition

The study of idioms originated in the 1960s and flourished in the 1980s and 1990s. Scholars conducted in-depth and detailed research on the classification of idioms, the characteristics of idioms, the variation of idioms, the construction of idioms, and the relationship between figurative and literal meanings of idioms from the perspectives of functional linguistics, formal linguistics, psycholinguistics, cognitive linguistics and pragmatics. Bruce Fraser (1970) proposed the frozenness hierarchy of idioms from the perspective of transformational generative grammar, dividing idioms into seven solidification levels to classify, but this classification does not cover all idioms. Chitra Fernando (1981) proposed the functionalization of idioms, arguing that one of the main functions of idioms is to assist in communication and express people's thoughts in an effective way. The Decomposition Model proposed by P. Nayak (1989) states that the meaning of idioms can be obtained by decomposition. R.W. Gibbs, Jr. et al. (1993, 1995) based on empirical research on the metaphor model, arguing that the metaphorical meaning of idioms is activated by a separate system of ideas that exists in our brains. Wang Ying (2007) proposed the Holistic Approach of English idioms suitable for non-native English speakers, which integrates the five elements of syntax, semantics, pragmatics, cognition, and social culture into an organic unity, providing theoretical guidance to learners, and the integrated processing method focuses on input to learners, but do students effectively learn idioms? The authors do not confirm this with empirical studies. In short, the research of these scholars focuses on studying idioms themselves, such as their characteristics, types, and structures, to help learners learn idioms, while ignoring the role of the learners themselves in the learning process. To learn and master English, the key is to study how learners learn idioms and how they learn more effectively. Based on previous empirical research, this chapter proposes the M-E-A-N model, the T-R-A-C-E model, and the S-S-P-C model of English idiom acquisition, aiming to explore how English as a foreign language learners learn English idioms more effectively.

9.1 Construction of M-E-A-N Model of English Idiom Acquisition

9.1.1 The Structure and Connotation of the M-E-A-N Model

For learners who use English as a foreign language, the M-E-A-N model of English idiom learning is composed of the acronyms of motivation, exploration, assessment, and need, which represent the four factors of learners' motivation, exploration, evaluation, and need. Motivation includes integrative motivation and instrumental motivation; Exploration includes analysis and discussion; Assessment include self-assessment, teacher assessment and peer evaluation; Need means achievement is needed. Learning motivation promotes exploration, after which assessment is needed. Assessment meets need, which pushes learning motivation. These four factors are interrelated and cyclical. The M-E-A-N model will be elaborated as follows:

1) M represents motivation, which can be divided into two types: integrative motivation and instrumental motivation. Integrative moti-

vation refers to learners who have knowledge or a special interest in the target language community and wish to interact or integrate into its social life. Instrumental motivation refers to learners who aim to obtain economic benefits or other benefits, such as passing an exam or obtaining a scholarship.

2) E represents exploration, which includes analysis and discussion. Due to cultural differences between different countries, to learn English well, second language learners need to have a good grasp of the culture of English-speaking countries. In the process of learning idioms, learners should actively and actively learn and analyze various types of idioms. When faced with problems, they should analyze and discuss the origin, characteristics, context, and meaning of idioms together, so that learning idioms is no longer a difficult problem.

3) A represents assessment, which includes self-assessment, teacher assessment, and peer assessment. Self-assessment mainly refers to learners' assessment of their own language learning; teacher assessment refers to the assessment of students' language learning by teachers; peer assessment mainly refers to mutual assessment among learners.

4) N represents need, which mainly refers to achievement needs, which include the pursuit of success and the desire for superiority and the need to do their best. The achievement need theory, also known as the "three needs theory", was proposed by David McClelland, a professor at Harvard University, through his research on human needs and motivation and was published in a series of articles in the 1950s. In the process of learning English idioms, learners can only further stimulate their learning motivation if they achieve their achievement needs.

9.1.2 The Rationale of the M-E-A-N Model and Its Application

In the process of acquiring English idioms, we can analyze and solve the difficulties encountered in idiom learning based on the four dimensions of the M-E-A-N model.

9.1.2.1 Motivation

For foreign language learners, despite studying English for more than a decade, it is still difficult to express native and fluent English, especially when learning idioms. Many learners do not pay attention to or even neglect learning idioms, thinking that learning English is just about memorizing words and grammar. However, idioms are commonly used in English-speaking countries. Cooper (1999) pointed out that an average adult native language speaker would say about 10 million metaphors and 20 million idioms in their lifetime. So how can learners master idioms well? Learners' previous misconceptions should be changed, and their motivation for learning should be fully mobilized. From the perspective of tool-type motivation, teachers should actively guide learners and emphasize the importance of learning idioms. According to the requirements of the teaching syllabus, students of different ages need to master different levels of idioms, and the assessment of idioms can be appropriately increased in exams to stimulate learners' learning desire. From the perspective of integrated motivation, the motivation to learn idioms comes from learners' intrinsic needs, interests, and motivation. In the Chinese context, most learners lack this motivation, so we need to consciously cultivate learners' emotional attachment to learning idioms to make them interested in it. In the process of learning English idioms, learners should have a positive emotion. The sayings "Interest is the best teacher" and "Love what you do" illustrate that we should fully mobilize our emotional factors in the learning process in order to effectively learn English. Many learners only pay attention to the vocabulary required for exams when learning English vocabulary, and fail to realize that idioms are an important part of vocabulary, so they adopt a negative attitude towards learning idioms without motivation and passion. Therefore, it is suggested that learners should also approach learning idioms with a positive attitude and emotional attachment in order to achieve better results with less effort.

9.1.2.2 Exploration

Idioms can be analyzed and discussed from different perspectives. Ferando (1996) proposed that idioms can be divided into pure idioms, semi-idioms, and literal idioms. From the perspective of transparency, Cacciari, C. & P. Tabossi (1991) divided idioms into transparent idioms and opaque idioms. Nippol (2002) found that adults have a better understanding of idioms than children, but idioms with the same level of transparency are equally easy for both children and adults to understand, and children and adults find it easier to understand idioms with higher transparency. Xie Hua (2007) believes that for learners, there is no clear correlation between transparency and understanding of idioms, but idioms with higher transparency are easier to understand. From the perspective of second language acquisition, Lauffer (2000) divided idioms into total formal similar idiom in semantics and form, partial formal similar idiom in semantics and form, different idioms in L1 (different semantic and forms but with the same conceptual metaphor), L1 non-idiom (L2 idioms that do not exist semantically or formally in L1 idioms). Understanding the characteristics and different classifications of idioms can deepen our understanding of idioms. At the same time, a large amount of research shows that context has an impact on the understanding of idioms. Tang Ling (2012) found through empirical investigations that learners' understanding of idioms is closely related to their ability to use context. It is easier to understand idioms with context than without context, and context is closely related to reading ability. Learners with strong reading ability can better understand the meaning of idioms based on context than those with poor reading ability. Nippold (1989) found through experiments with and without context that learners' accuracy in learning idioms is higher with context than without context.

Firstly, from the perspective of idiom transparency, idioms can be transparent or opaque. For example: *kill two birds with one stone*, according to its literal meaning "one stone kills two birds" , which is easy to remind us of Chinese idiom "*yì shí èr niǎo*" , so we can say this type of idioms is transparent idiom; The counterpart is the opaque idiom, which means that the idiom has a long diachronic background and is not easy to understand. For example, *he eats no fish and plays the game*. It is wrong to interpret it literally as "He doesn't eat fish and plays games" . This idiom originated in the Elizabethan era when English Catholics who followed Roman Catholic regulations were required to only eat fish and not meat on Fridays, which were designated as "fish day," by the English Catholic Church. However, English Protestants refused to follow this Roman Catholic custom as a sign of loyalty to the government and continued to eat meat on Fridays. Thus, the idiom "He eats no fish" which originally referred to one's loyalty to Protestantism, evolved to mean "loyal." Similarly, "to play the game" came to mean "to be straightforward and honest". In the process of learning English idioms, learners may encounter transparent and opaque idioms. While transparent idioms can be easily learned, opaque idioms require learners to break them down into simpler, understandable components. Teachers should not simply introduce the basic meaning of opaque idioms, but also provide the etymology and background to help students understand their origins and deepen their impressions of these idioms. Furthermore, students must take the initiative to learn on their own outside of class and seek additional resources when encountering phrases or sentences they do not understand. With a positive attitude and a lot of practice, students can overcome the challenges of learning idioms.

Secondly, there are many types of English idioms, which can be compared and categorized based on their transparency, familiarity, cultural differences, etc. For example, idioms related to colors, animals, body parts, time, weather, etc. can be classified separately, and then analyzed according to the cultural differences between the East and the West. This not only facilitates the learning of idioms but also enriches students' cultural knowledge and deepens their understanding of English vocabulary, laying a solid foundation for better English learning. Liu Hongli (2007) pointed out that there are similarities and differences in the expression of color words between English and Chinese, and it is necessary to pay attention to these differences in the process of learning English to avoid misunderstandings. Meanwhile, Wang Shibin (1999) suggested that different types of words should be categorized for association memory to achieve better learning effects. For example, in English, yellow is associated with jealousy, cowardice, and badness, while in China, it is often associated with pornography. Hence, idiomatic expressions related to colors in English and Chinese are different. For example, in English, yellow is associated with jealousy, cowardice, and corruption. In American slang "cowards" are called yellow belly; Yellow is used in China to refer to pornography, such as pornographic magazines and pornographic causes, while in English blue films are used to refer to pornographic films. Besides, yellow is also a symbol of Chinese national culture. In international political groups, yellow represents liberals.

Finally, in learning idioms, we can start by understanding the context and classifying idioms according to their acquisition in second language learning. We can study different types of idioms in a systematic way. Firstly, idioms that have a complete semantic and formal equivalence and idioms that only have some semantic and formal equivalence are easy for second language learners to acquire. For example, idioms without context like *make sb.' s hair curl/ stand on end* can be easily understood as "make someone' s hair curly". However, when used in context like *the clothes some young people wear nowadays really make your hair cur*, the meaning can easily be misunderstood. Therefore, by understanding the context, we may guess that the young people's dressing sends chills down the spine and can be understood as "the dressing of modern young people is really scary". Secondly, idioms that have different semantic and formal expressions but have the same underlying metaphors and L2 idioms that do not exist in L1 idioms either semantically or formally, are also considered as vague idioms. For example, the Chinese idiom "ben mo dao zhi (putting the cart before the horse)" originated from the fact that China was an agricultural country, where farming was considered more important than commerce. Some people who did not engage in farming but rather commerce was looked down upon. This idiom metaphorically means reversing the positions of important and trivial things. However, in English, the same idiom is translated as "put the cart before the horse", which also means reversing the order of things. "Not worth one's salt" means "ineffective" or "unable to carry out one's duties", which originates from the Latin word "salarium", meaning the money given to Roman soldiers to buy salt, rather than for the purpose of buying salt. If a person's value was not worth the cost of the salt they consumed, then they were considered worthless. In an interview, there was a question: "Is food worth its salt?" and many students misunderstood it as a question about the relationship between food and salt or whether something was worth doing. This highlights the difficulties faced by second language learners in comprehending idioms without context. Therefore, we can conclude that context is a crucial factor in the acquisition and comprehension of idioms by language learners.

Through the examples given above, we can understand that we need to learn to analyze idioms based on their types, characteristics, and the different meanings they can express in various contexts. We can also discuss the origins and meanings of idioms with other learners or tutors to fully understand them. This method can save time and improve our learning efficiency.

9.1.2.3 Assessment

For learners whose English is a foreign language, regular and quantitative assessment is a must. After gradually analyzing idioms and understanding their origins and meanings, learners need to practice and memorize them extensively. This learning method, which involves reviewing the old and learning the new while repeating and practicing, is critical for learners in China who do not have a conducive learning environment with only limited class time. Thus, learners must also engage in extracurricular learning, and both in-class and out-of-class learning should be combined with corresponding assessment to promote their development. Self-assessment, teacher assessment, and peer assessment are the three aspects of assessment that can be used to promote progress in learning. Self-assessment involves learners' giving themselves timely feedback on their understanding of idioms or their performance in related exercises and identifying their shortcomings or setting new goals. Teacher assessment involves teachers guiding and evaluating learners by assigning a specific quantity of idiom homework and periodically conducting assessments in the classroom or after class. Peer evaluation involves learners engaging in group discussions to assess and evaluate each other's learning, and groups can also hold discussions or competitions to promote interaction and communication among learners and to ensure that evaluation is integrated into the learning process with the aim of promoting learning.

9.1.2.4 Need

According to the requirements of the National College English Teaching Syllabus, the number of idioms students of different grade levels are expected to master varies, and the requirements for idiom mastery progress gradually from the first to the fourth year, reflecting the need for achievement. Achievement needs are stable and enduring motivating factors for contemporary college students seeking knowledge and success, and they occupy a primary position among the various needs of college students. From the first to the fourth year, learners face different learning goals regarding idioms, and they must first establish confidence to overcome these challenges. Confidence is a powerful driver for completing a task. Learners facing difficulties in the process of learning idioms must encourage themselves constantly and seek help from teachers and classmates, solving problems together. Furthermore, learners working towards their needs for achievement must assign themselves tasks and use online resources to assist their learning. When they reach their learning goals for a stage, they have fulfilled the achievement needs for that stage, which motivates them to work towards their next goals and sustains their learning motivation, ultimately forming a virtuous cycle to achieve their final learning goals.

9.1.3 Summary

The learning process for English idioms should focus on the M-E-A-N model, in which, M stands for Motivation, E stands for Exploring, A stands for Assessment, and N stands for Need. According to the M-E-A-N model, English learners should do as follows:

1) During the process of learning idioms, students may encounter some uncommon ones. They should try their best to make these vague idioms become clear by using context and analyzing and summarizing their forms, turning them into transparent idioms for memory retention. Through repeated practice, the process of M-E-A-N becomes a cycle, integrated and interconnected. Learners of English idioms should make full use of this model to create a positive and good learning environment, making the learning of English idioms more effective and hence firmly mastering English.

2) Outside of class, students should learn to use this learning model to learn idioms when they encounter them. Students can watch more English original movies, read English magazines, and listen to slow-paced recordings, which will unconsciously increase their correct input of idioms. Only with correct input can idioms be correctly output.

3) Learners should have a positive attitude in the learning process of English idioms, solving the difficulties encountered in learning with optimism and actively pursuing learning, continuously developing their thinking abilities, and learning to think and analyze problems in order to truly master English idioms.

9.2 Construction of T-R-A-C-E Model of English Idiom Acquisition

T-R-A-C-E model consists of five aspects. In the name of the model of T-R-A-C-E, the five alphabets T, R, A, C, E respectively stands for transparency, repetition, analysis, culture and emotion.

9.2.1 The Structure and Connotation of the T-R-A-C-E Model

9.2.1.1 The Alphabet T Stands for Transparency

According to the categorization of idiom transparency by Cacciari and Tabossi, idioms can be divided into transparent idioms and opaque idioms. Transparent idioms refer to idioms whose literal meaning or the literal meaning of their components is closely related to their figurative meaning. Opaque idioms refer to idioms whose literal meaning and figurative meaning are not closely related. It is an extension of a literal idiom. For example, "wolf in sheep's clothing" literally means "a wolf wearing sheepskin", which has the same meaning as the Chinese idiom "*pī zhe yáng pí de láng*", describing hypocrites who are treacherous inside; "as poor as a mouse" literally means "as poor as a mouse". We all know that there is nothing to eat in the church, so the teachers in the church must not have anything to eat. By inference, we can conclude that the mice in the church are very poor, making it easy to understand that the meaning of this idiom is "penniless" or "dirt poor". These are all transparent idioms, where there is a close connection between the literal meaning and the figurative meaning, making it easy for learners to acquire.

Opaque idioms, on the other hand, are difficult to infer the meaning from the literal meaning of the words, and students need to master the cultural and historical background of a language to understand their meaning. For example, "let the cat out of the bag" literally means "let the cat run out of the bag". If its origin is not understood, it will definitely be misunderstood. The actual meaning of this idiom is "to reveal a secret". It is said to originate from ancient England. At the time, pig sellers would put pigs in bags for easy transportation. Buyers would usually trust that the bag contained a pig and would not check again. Some dishonest sellers would put cats or dogs in the bags, deceiving customers, thus giving rise to this idiom. "White elephant" literally means "white elephant", but it has a different meaning. The story behind this idiom is that Thailand was originally called Siam and has been known for producing elephants since ancient times. However, white elephants are very rare and are considered sacred animals. Any white elephant born must be owned by the king, and it is explicitly stated that no one is allowed to use white elephants, otherwise they will be punished by law. Legend has it that in ancient Siam, there was a king who was dissatisfied with a certain minister and gave him a white elephant as a gift. This white elephant was extremely valuable, considered sacred, and was given by the king, so it could not be bought, sold, or transferred. Therefore, the minister had to bear the heavy financial burden of raising it, eventually ruining his own wealth. According to this legend, the term "white elephant" evolved to mean "something that consumes a lot of resources but has no practical value, and something that is burdensome and a liability". Its underlying meaning cannot be inferred from its literal meaning alone. Therefore, when faced with opaque idioms, we must do more research, and after understanding the origin of the idiom, memorizing it will become much easier. Adults have a stronger understanding of idioms with low transparency, whereas children and adults have similar understanding abilities for idioms with the same transparency level.

9.2.1.2 The Alphabet R Stands for Repetition

Repetition means the continuous and repetitive practice in the process of learning idioms. Only through continuous repetition can one firmly master idioms. As mentioned above, second language learners lack a language environment for learning. How can this deficiency be made up for? Only through their own repeated practice can they truly master idioms. However, it should be pointed out that this kind of repetitive practice is not blind memorization, but should be based on the various characteristics of idioms and various strategies should be used for repeated practice in order to achieve the goal of truly mastering idioms.

9.2.1.3 The Alphabet A Stands for Analysis

Analysis means we should be good at analyzing, summarizing, and generalizing in the process of learning. For English language learners, in order to master English idioms, the essence of the English language, they must further learn English idioms by analyzing the structural, semantic, and formal characteristics of idioms. When we encounter various idioms, we can classify them according to categories. For example, by categorizing idioms according to their themes, various thematic idioms can be classified accordingly. By categorizing idioms according to their sources, there are idioms related to historical allusions, mythology, Aesop's fables, animals, plants, economics, politics, family life, religious culture, classic literature works, etc. Additionally, idioms can be classified according to familiarity, transparency, semantic decomposition strategies, and cultural differences. Analyzing various types of idioms can help second language learners to deepen their understanding and mastery of idioms. Furthermore, we can analyze the meaning of idioms through context. Context refers to the linguistic environment, which includes language factors as well as non-language factors such as the context, time, space, situation, object, discourse premise, etc. that are related to word usage. A large amount of research has shown that context has an impact on the understanding of idioms. Empirical survey results indicate that regardless of the proficiency level of the learner and the difficulty of the idiom, it is easier to understand idioms with context than without context.

Nippold conducted an experiment in two modes on learners and found that the accuracy rate of learning idioms is higher with context than without context. For example, "eating one's words" easily reminds people of the Chinese idiom "*shí yán*" (to eat one's words), because these two phrases are matching in both structure and literal meaning. However, "eating one's words" means retracting what one has said, acknowledging that the previous words were wrong, and carries a certain emotional color, which is a shameful and discreditable admission of error. But it is much easier to understand the meaning of this idiom in a certain context. For example, "Lily, I'm really embarrassed that I have to eat my words. The money I expected to receive last week didn't arrive." When this context is given, it is easy to guess the meaning of the idiom based on the meaning before and after, which means "to retract what one has said." Another example is "fat chance". In a contextless situation, we might easily mistake it for "a lot of opportunities" because "fat" means "fat, obese," which easily conveys the meaning of "many." However, in this case, "fat" means "rarely or not at all," so this idiom means "no chance, very unlikely." In a contextual situation, such as "A fat chance I'll ever get a good grade in physics or chemistry; I'm just not very good when it comes to science. Maybe I ought to major in history or journalism instead," we can easily guess the meaning of "fat chance" based on the explanation in the sentence, which means "almost impossible."

9.2.1.4 The Alphabet C Stands for Culture

Culture is a very broad and highly humanistic concept, and providing an accurate or precise definition of culture is indeed a very difficult task. Narrowly defined, culture refers to people's common social habits, such as living, dressing, customs, lifestyles, and behavioral norms. Boers & Demecheleer's research shows that the understanding of second language learners and native speakers is different. Learners are influenced by cultural differences between their mother tongue and second language when they understand idioms. They also found that learners rely more on context to understand low-transparent idioms and use semantic decomposition strategies to understand high-transparent idioms. For idioms with the same culture between China and the West, we can easily acquire them. However, for idioms with cultural differences between China and the West, we must carefully search for information to find the cultural origins of the idioms in order to learn them better. English idioms are mainly derived from ancient Greek mythology, Aesop's fables, ancient Roman legends, biblical references, religious beliefs, and cultural classics. For example, "to rest on one's laurels" means complacency, and Laurel is a type of evergreen tree that is used for ornamental purposes. "Laurels" refers to a "crown" made of bay leaves. According to legend, in ancient Greek Roman mythology, Apollo, the sun god's lover—Daphne, was turned into a laurel tree by her father, the river god. Since then, every time Apollo sees a laurel tree, he cannot help but think of her, and he loves the laurel tree. Therefore, ancient Greeks retained a tradition that the winners of sports competitions were awarded the laurel wreath to show their respect for Apollo. This trend gradually spread throughout Europe, so laurels represent victory, success, and distinction. English and American cultures are influenced by Christian culture, and people believe in Christianity, with the Bible being their must-read book. Therefore, there are many English idioms related to it. Idioms related to God are as follows: "God helps those who help themselves," "God sends fortune to fools" "go to hell" "God's mill goes slowly, but it grinds fine" "God is above all" "God is where he was" "God bless me" "for God's sake" "Nature does nothing in vain" "Man proposes, God disposes" and "God resists the proud, but gives grace to the humble." Language contains culture. Due to cultural differences between countries, it is necessary to have a good grasp of the culture of English-speaking countries in order to learn English well.

Second language learners should actively learn and analyze various types of idioms during the learning process. By comparing and analyzing different idioms, second language learners can make language learning no longer a difficult problem.

9.2.1.5 The Alphabet E Stands for Emotion

Emotion means that learners need to have a positive attitude during the process of learning English idioms. Throughout the process of learning English idioms, it is important to maintain a positive and optimistic attitude. When faced with difficulties, we should not make assumptions or guess randomly. Instead, we should actively seek information or ask teachers or classmates for help based on the context to study idioms more effectively. Only in this way can we learn idioms effectively. For example, in English movies, we often hear the expression "Watch my six". Although each word in this phrase is simple, we may not understand its specific meaning. This is where we should actively think and analyze: if a person stands at the center of a clock face, 12 o'clock can be understood as the front, 3 o'clock as the right 90 degrees, 9 o'clock as the left 90 degrees, and 6 o'clock as the rear. In fact, "watch my six" is a phrase related to the position of clock hands, which is not related to numbers or time, but means "look behind me".

9.2.2 Implications

During the process of learning English idioms, it is important to focus on the mode of T-R-A-C-E, with T representing transparency of idioms, R referring to the repetition of learning idioms, A representing the process of analyzing and summarizing idioms, C indicating the cultural aspects of learning idioms, and E symbolizing the need to have positive attitudes when learning idioms.

1) In the process of acquiring idioms, second language learners should closely follow the mode of TRACE to learn idioms according to the characteristics of English idioms. Second language learners should learn to analyze the transparency and familiarity of the idioms, pay attention to and learn about the culture of English-speaking countries, and practice learning idioms with a positive attitude. Only by persevering in learning can they gradually learn a large number of English idioms. Additionally, second language learners can use comparative analysis to classify and summarize idioms based on the similarities and differences between their mother tongue and English idioms.

2) The T-R-A-C-E model is a circular and comprehensive model that should be used by teachers in the teaching process of English idioms. Teachers should create a positive and good learning environ-

ment for learners to effectively learn idioms. For example, teachers can classify idioms based on their transparency and difficulty level. For difficult idioms, teachers can provide context to help students understand the meaning and usage of the idioms. Learners can also learn idioms through retelling, paraphrasing, and playing games. Furthermore, teachers should cultivate learners' abilities to flexibly use English idioms.

3) Learning English idioms is not a one-time thing, and it requires the attention and efforts of both teachers and learners. Only with a positive attitude and a serious approach can learners effectively learn English idioms.

9.3 Construction of S-S-P-C Model of English Idiom Acquisition

9.3.1 The Theoretical Construction of S-S-P-C Model

As mentioned earlier, there have been two major views in the field of psycholinguistics regarding the understanding of idioms: the non-compositional view and the compositional view. As research has progressed, most scholars have come to embrace the compositional view. While it may seem difficult to infer the meaning of idioms from their constituent parts, there is some degree of connection between the constituent parts and the meaning of the idioms. These connections have become obscured over time due to historical and linguistic changes. As a result, on the basis of the compositional view of idioms, we have developed the S-S-P-C model for understanding English idioms. This model involves decomposing and analyzing idioms from four aspects: syntax, semantics, pragmatics, and culture, allowing English learners to deeply understand and flexibly use idioms using this model. The model can be depicted graphically as follows:

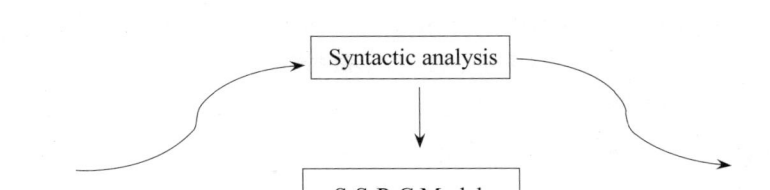

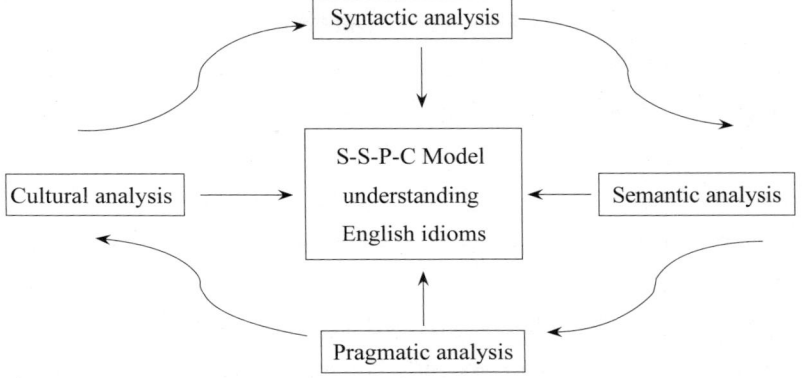

```
                    ┌─────────────────┐
                    │ Syntactic analysis │
                    └─────────────────┘
                             │
                             ▼
┌──────────────┐    ┌─────────────────┐    ┌──────────────┐
│ Cultural analysis │ ──▶│   S-S-P-C Model │◀── │ Semantic analysis │
│              │    │   understanding  │    │              │
│              │◀── │  English idioms  │    │              │
└──────────────┘    └─────────────────┘    └──────────────┘
                             ▲
                             │
                    ┌─────────────────┐
                    │ Pragmatic analysis │
                    └─────────────────┘
```

Chart 9-1 S-S-P-C Model of English Idiom Acquisition

9.3.1.1 Syntactic Perspective

English idioms are composed of two or more words that are combined according to certain grammatical rules. When English learners comprehend and acquire idioms, they need to analyze the syntactic structure of the idiom to understand its grammatical function. Idioms can be divided into three categories: clause idioms, phrase idioms, and sentence idioms. Clause idioms, also known as predicate phrases, have verbs as their first words and have the syntactic function of a verb in a sentence. They mainly serve as predicates in a sentence, such as "come alive" "break the ice" "drive someone mad" "do someone a favor" "burn the candle at both ends" "miss the boat", etc. Among them, the predicate phrase structure can be further divided into verb + complement, verb + object, verb + object + complement, verb + object + direct object, verb + object + modifier. English idioms with the structure of "verb + complement" include "be the bee's knees" "bend over backward" "bolt to the bran" "bleed to death" , and so on. The English idioms with the structure of "verb + object" include "addle one's brain" "achieve one's end" "bate one's breath" "blow one's cover" "burn one's fingers" , and so on. The idioms with the structure of "verb + object + complement" include "blood someone white" "catch someone red-handed" "catch sb tripping" "drive sb round the bend" , and so on. English idioms with the structure of "verb + indirect object + direct object" include "do sb. an injustice" "drop someone a line" "deal someone a blow" "give the devil his due" , and so on. The English idioms with the structure of "verb + object + modifier" include "avoid something like the plague" "blow something sky-high" "burn the candle at both ends" "carry something too far" , and so on.

  Phrase idioms that are not verbs, also known as non-predicate phrases, do not have the syntactic function of a verb and cannot serve as predicates. These idioms can be further divided into noun phrase idioms, which have a noun as their center or key word and can serve as a noun in a sentence, such as "a big fish in a little pond" "wolf whistles" "yellow dog" ; adjective phrase idioms, which serve as adjectives in a sentence, although their constituents are not necessarily all adjectives, such as "quick as lightning" "as busy as a bee" "as cool as a cucumber" ; prepositional phrase idioms, which are equivalent to a preposition in a sentence, such as "at wit's end" "between you and me" "beyond all measure" ; adverb phrase idioms, which are equivalent to an adverb in a sentence, such as "full steam ahead" "heart and soul" "hand in glove" ; and phrase idioms with repeated or contrasting constituents, such as "odds and ends" "body and soul" "bread and circuses" "cash and carry" "cut and dry" , and so on.

Sentence idioms are either omitted or complete sentences, mainly in the form of proverbs, moral sayings, and so on. In terms of sentence types, there are declarative sentences, interrogative sentences, imperative sentences, and exclamatory sentences. From the perspective of simple and complex sentences, there are simple sentences, compound sentences, and complex sentences, such as "A good beginning is half done. Better late than never. All men by nature desire knowledge", and so on. These syntactic classifications of English idioms are very helpful for students to understand and acquire them. When learning an idiom, students need to analyze its syntactic structure and classify it according to the above methods. On the one hand, classifying idioms can organize seemingly chaotic idioms to help students memorize their spellings in bulk; on the other hand, it helps students grasp the syntactic functions of idioms, because idioms with different structures have different syntactic functions, and idiom classification is in a sense analyzing their syntactic functions. The root cause of syntactic errors when using idioms lies in not analyzing their syntactic structure. Once the syntactic classification of idioms is completed, their syntactic functions become self-evident. Therefore, when acquiring English idioms, learners need to adopt a syntactic analysis approach.

9.3.1.2 Semantic Perspective

Semantically speaking, semantics is at the core of idioms. The primary aspect of understanding and acquiring idioms is understanding and acquiring their semantics, which is the idiomatic meaning or metaphorical meaning, rather than the literal meaning. The semantic analysis of idioms can help learners understand the metaphorical meanings of idioms. There are three characteristics of idiom semantics: holism, transparency (decomposability), and specificity.

Holism is an important feature of idioms, which refers to the fact that idiom semantics are indivisible wholes, as they are constructions whose meaning is not simply the literal sum of its constituent parts, but rather achieved through their combination. Supporters of the holistic view of idiom semantics argue that the meaning of idioms cannot be derived from the literal meaning of the constituent parts, and they can only be learned through rote memorization. In fact, both idiom semantics and their constituent parts have systematic conceptual correspondences. For example, "black sheep" does not literally mean a "black horse", but rather conveys the meaning of "a person who brings shame or embarrassment to a family or group". This is because in Western culture, black sheep are viewed as less valuable than white sheep because their wool is difficult to dye. Hence, if a family's herd contains a black sheep, it is considered bad luck, and this gradually came to mean a family member who is a disgrace or outcast, figuratively referred to as the "black sheep".

Transparency, also known as decomposability, refers to the degree to which the literal meanings of the constituent parts contribute to the metaphorical meaning of the idiom as a whole. High-transparency idioms have a close link between their literal and figurative meanings, making it easier to infer the figurative meaning from the literal one, whereas low-transparency idioms have a loose or even nonexistent link between their literal and figurative meanings, which makes it more difficult to infer the figurative meaning from the literal one. For high-transparency idioms such as "long time no see", which means "it's been a while since we last saw each other", the meaning can be inferred from the literal meaning. For semi-transparent idioms such as "cast pearls before swine", which literally means "to display jewels in front of a pig", but figuratively means "to offer something valuable to someone who is incapable of appreciating it", the metaphorical meaning is more difficult to understand and requires an understanding of the underlying meaning. Non-transparent idioms, such as "carry a torch for somebody", meaning "to have an unrequited love for someone", are more difficult to infer from the literal meaning. However, such idioms with no relation between literal and figurative meanings are relatively rare, and most idioms have some traceable link between literal and figurative meanings.

Specificity manifests in two forms: semantics that violate logic and semantics that are not classifiable by analogy. The former refers to semantics that contradict logic, while the latter refers to semantics that cannot be inferred by analogy. The meaning of idioms cannot be deduced based on logical common sense. For example, the idiom "kick the bucket" means "to die", and "face the music" means "to take responsibility for one's mistake". Both of these idioms cannot be inferred based on logical common sense.

We can use the theory of cognitive semantics to infer idiomatic or metaphorical meanings of idioms, since idiom semantics are closely connected to cognition, and we can infer the metaphorical meaning of idioms based on the underlying cognitive category. Therefore, the acquisition of idioms, using semantic analysis to obtain idiomatic or metaphorical meanings, is the most important sign of success in idiom acquisition.

9.3.1.3 Pragmatic Perspective

From a pragmatic perspective, understanding the pragmatic meaning of idioms is also an important aspect of successfully acquiring idioms. Failure to understand the pragmatic use of idioms can lead to communication failure and even significant misunderstandings between communicators. Chinese English learners often make pragmatic errors when using idioms, including linguistic and social pragmatic errors. These errors have their own underlying reasons.

Chinese English learners often find that even though their English oral or written skills are very fluent, they still encounter obstacles in cross-cultural communication. The key to this problem lies in the lack of pragmatic ability. When Chinese English learners understand English idioms, they should also pay attention to their pragmatic meaning, including the stylistic and emotional colors of idioms, which determine the context in which the idioms are used. Different stylistic and emotional colors of idioms require different contexts or situations and objects for application. Chinese English learners need to choose the appropriate idioms based on the context. For example, the idioms "look down upon" and "look down one's nose at" have a similar literal meaning of "to disdain or look down upon someone" , but their usage and connotations are vastly different. The former is a neutral term with a wider range of applicable contexts, while the latter is an informal and colloquial expression that is only appropriate in informal conversations.

In idioms, some rhetorical devices are often used to make the language more vivid and powerful, such as metaphor, personification, exaggeration, and parallelism. Many simile idioms, such as "as clear as crystal," "as light as a feather," "as brave as a lion," and "as poor as a church mouse," express the speaker's attitude or viewpoint towards the described "person" or "thing" , which is an exaggerated way of expression. There are also metaphorical idioms, such as "He has a heart of stone" . In this case, "heart" and "stone" have no necessary connection and belong to two different things. However, using "stone" to metaphorize "heart" emphasizes how hard-hearted the person is.

There are also idioms used for social communication, such as "How's everything going?" "How are you?" "See you then." "Have a good time." "Can I help you?" In daily life, people mainly use these idioms to establish and maintain friendly interpersonal relationships or social contacts. Just like how Chinese people often say "Have you eaten? Where are you going?" when they meet each other. The pragmatic function of these idioms is social.

For Chinese English learners, paying attention to the pragmatic meaning of idioms when comprehending and acquiring them is an indispensable and important aspect. However, most students and teachers overlook this point, which must be taken seriously. When English learners acquire idioms, if they adopt a pragmatic analysis method, they can obtain the pragmatic usage of idioms, avoid pragmatic errors, and acquire idioms in a well-rounded way and use them appropriately in appropriate contexts.

9.3.1.4 Cultural Perspective

Culturally speaking, language and culture are inseparable. As the essence of a national language, idioms have distinct national features. Idioms in various languages reflect their respective national cultures, which have been developed over thousands of years. Language reflects culture, and culture is an important source of language. Many idioms are closely related to culture. Different ethnic groups have cultural differences, and their idioms carry their own cultural characteristics. Native English speakers are familiar with their own culture, making it effortless for them to understand idioms with their own cultural characteristics. However, Chinese English learners lack English cultural background knowledge, which makes it difficult for them to learn these

English idioms. As second language learners, Chinese students can understand and learn idioms at a higher level if they deepen their knowledge of their own culture and become familiar with English-speaking countries' culture, as well as understand some idioms' cultural origins or sources.

For example, there are many idioms in English related to "dogs," such as "Every dog has its day" and "Love me, love my dog," in which "dog" represents loyalty and carries a positive connotation. However, in Chinese culture, "dog" conveyed by "*quǎn*" or "*gǒu*" is often used negatively, such as in "*sàng jiā zhī quǎn*" which means "a stray dog" or in "*gǒu pì bù tōng*" which means "nonsense" . In addition, Eastern and Western people have different understandings of "dragon" . Chinese people consider the dragon as a sacred animal, and they consider themselves descendants of the dragon, while Westerners regard the dragon as a monster, an intimidating creature. Many English idioms come from Greek mythology and biblical references, such as "Achilles' heel", which means "fatal flaw or weakness." This idiom comes from a Greek myth. Achilles is a warrior, and his mother soaked him in the River Styx as a baby to obtain invincibility for him. However, because she held him by his ankles, his ankles were not submerged and became his weak point. During the Trojan War, he was immune to attacks due to the river's blessing, but Paris shot him with an arrow in his ankle, which caused his death. Since then, people have used this idiom to describe "weakness" or "fatal flaw." Moreover, Westerners have strong religious beliefs, especially in Christianity, which gives rise to many idioms related to God and the Bible, such as "blind God" "My God!" "depart to God" "Good God!" and "He that serves God for money will serve the devil for better wages." Understanding the cultural difference between China and the West is essential to comprehending and using English idioms with cultural characteristics effectively. Analyzing and comprehending idioms from a cultural perspective is an essential method for learning them.

9.3.2 The Empirical Research of S-S-P-C Mode

9.3.2.1 Pre-test and a Group Interview

Before beginning the teaching experiment of S-S-P-C model, we conducted a pre-test and a group interview. We chose college students as subjects. The students, who were non-English majors, were sophomores from Guangxi National Normal University for Nationalities. The students' majors cover Chinese majors, Law majors, Physics majors, Chemistry majors, and so on. All students from ten classes participated in the pre-text. Forty-two students were from Class One, which would be the contrastive class, and forty students were from Class Two, which would be the teaching experiment class. The number of students from Class Three to Ten ranged from forty to forty-three. We chose forty English idioms randomly from *Oxford Dictionary of Idioms* edited by Judith Siefring as the material for the pre-text. The forty English idioms were not included in the subjects' textbooks. The subjects were expected to translate the English idioms into Chinese. If an idiom was translated correctly, the subject would score 2.5 marks, or else he would score zero. The scores were analyzed by SPSS 17.0. Ten classes' scores of English idiom test are displayed in Table 9-1.

Table 9-1 Ten Classes' Scores of English Idiom Test

Class	N	Mean	Std. Deviation	Std. Error	95% Confidence Interval for Mean	
					Lower Bound	Upper Bound
1	42	29.10	14.062	2.170	24.71	33.48

Continued

Class	N	Mean	Std. Deviation	Std. Error	95% Confidence Interval for Mean Lower Bound	95% Confidence Interval for Mean Upper Bound
2	40	33.35	15.448	2.443	28.41	38.29
3	43	36.95	15.933	2.430	32.05	41.86
4	41	35.51	16.078	2.511	30.44	40.59
5	41	32.56	14.342	2.240	28.03	37.09
6	43	31.47	14.494	2.210	27.00	35.93
7	43	29.09	12.939	1.973	25.11	33.08
8	41	35.12	15.603	2.437	30.20	40.05
9	41	33.49	15.611	2.438	28.56	38.42
10	43	31.16	13.327	2.032	27.06	35.26
Total	418	32.76	14.862	.727	31.33	34.19

Table 9-1 shows that average scores of each class range from 30 to 35. The average scores of scores of Class 1, which will be the contrastive class, are 29.10; Std. Deviation is 14.062; Std. Error is 2.170; Lower Bound of 95% Confidence Interval for Mean is 24.71; Upper Bound is 33.48. In contrast, Class 2 will be the teaching experiment class, and its average scores are 33.35; Std. Deviation is 15.448; Std. Error is 2.443; Lower Bound of 95% Confidence Interval for Mean is 28.41; Upper Bound is 38.29. The low average score of English idioms test indicates that students from the ten classes are very poor in English idioms learning, including the would-be contrastive class and the teaching experiment class. In order to examine whether there were significant differences in English idiom learning between the ten classes, we conducted test of homogeneity of variances and one-way Analysis of Variance (Anova).

Table 9-2 Homogeneity Test for Variance

Levene Statistic	df1	df2	Sig.
1.361	9	408	.204

In Table 9-2, which is the result of the test of homogeneity of variances, P=.204>0.05, which shows that the data is suitable for one-way anova.

Table 9-3 One-Way ANOVA

	Sum of Squares	df	Mean Square	F	Sig.
Between Groups	2656.808	9	295.201	1.347	.211
Within Groups	89445.788	408	219.230		
Total	92102.596	417			

The one-way Anova in Table 9-3 shows that P=.211>0.05, which demonstrates that there is no significance difference between different groups.

The pre-test shows that college students from the ten classes are poor in English idiom learning and there is no significance difference between different classes, which lays a foundation for our further study.

In order to know the ins and outs of students' acquiring English idioms, we conducted a group interview. Six students among teaching experiment class were chosen randomly to be interviewed. The interviewed questions are: Do you think English idioms are more difficult than words? How do you learn English idioms?

About the first question, all the interviewed students admitted that English idioms were much harder to learn than English words and they felt frustrated about idioms learning. As to the second question, students gave different replies, which are transcribed as follows:

Student A: I have no special methods. When I learn English words, I try to memorize their spellings and their equivalent Chinese meanings by rote learning. I think idioms are just like words, so I adopt the same methods.

Student B: I have no special methods, either. An English idiom has an equivalent Chinese meaning. I have to memorize it just like a word. For example, put across, one meaning of which is to express, is just like a word. I cannot get its meaning by adding the meaning of "put" with the meaning of "across", so I have to remember that "put across" means "express", and I use the idiom "put across" in a sentence just like I use the word "express".

Student C: Idioms are special, which are somewhat different from words. For some idioms, I learn them by rote learning, such as "pick up" "bring up" "put across", each of which is a single unit, just like a word. For some idioms, I can link them to other things. For example, "be the last straw" is an interesting idiom. When I come across it, I remember that there is a nearly same saying in Chinese, so I conclude that it must be the same meaning as the saying in Chinese. However, this sort of idioms is not many; moreover, sometimes an English idiom has a completely different meaning from that seemingly similar Chinese equivalent, such as "eat one's words", which is nearly the same as "Shi Yan". "Eat one's words" means that "confess that one's predictions were wrong", which is completely different from "*shí yán*" with the meaning of "someone failed to do what is promised". So, I think rote learning is the best method, which can guarantee the meanings of idioms are understood as it should be.

Student D: I cannot agree with Student C more. Sometimes I speculate there may be a better way to learn idioms, and I try to link the English idiom with the Chinese idiom. Sometimes I can guess the meanings of some English idioms, but sometimes not. When I make a mistake, I am at a loss. So, I would rather learn idioms by rote learning, which is safe.

Student E: Learning idioms by rote learning are actually safe, but it is boring. We cannot remember so many things only by rote learning. I tried to find out some convenient and efficient method, but I failed. I expect maybe there is not such a method.

Student F: Actually, idioms learning is important, and I learn them by rote learning. However, when I come across a new idiom, I have to look up it in a dictionary, which makes me fail to concentrate on the story what I am reading. I am eager for an efficient idioms learning method.

From the interview transcriptions, we can make a summary about what students think of English idiom acquisition: English idioms are important, which should be attached great importance; An idiom is just like a word, which can be learned only like a word by rote learning; For English idiom acquisition, there are not an efficient method.

According to the pre-test and the interview, we can get to know the current situation about students' English idiom comprehending and acquisition: Chinese college students have great difficulties in comprehending and acquiring English idioms. They always acquire English idioms by adopting the traditional method—rote learning. They are not interested in English idioms and often avoid using idioms in both oral communication and written communication. They need some new English idiom acquisition methods badly.

9.3.2.2 The Application of S-S-P-C Model in College English Teaching

After the pre-test and the group interview, we began a teaching experiment. The teaching experiment lasted for one semester. We chose Class 2 as the teaching experiment class, and Class 1 as the contrastive class. In the teaching experiment class, there are 40 students, who major in Chinese. In the contrastive class, there are 42 students, who major in Chemistry. In the contrastive class, we adopted traditional teaching method. In other words, we attached no importance to English idiom teaching and acquisition, and we spent very little time on it or taught students to remember spellings and usages of those idioms as words. In the teaching experiment, we adopted the S-S-P-C model of English idiom acquisition. In other words, both the teacher and the students attached great importance to English idiom acquisition, and they saw idioms as special language elements. Specifically, the teacher taught idioms from the four perspectives: syntactic, semantic, pragmatic, and cultural.

The following is the procedure of teaching an idiom.

We take the idiom *carry coals to Newcastle* as an example. When teaching *carry coals to Newcastle*, the teacher instructs the students to analyze its syntactic structure. From the syntactic perspective, *carry coals to Newcastle* belongs to clause idioms and can be subcategorized into the pattern of Verb + Direct Object + adjunct. Therefore, the students can grasp grammatical usages of *carry coals to Newcastle*. In other words, the students will use it as a verb in a sentence instead of a noun. From the semantic perspective, the teacher analyzes its semantic meaning. The key word in this idiom is *Newcastle*, which is famous for boasting of lots of coals. The teacher tells students this knowledge and instructs students to speculate its semantic meaning from "carry coals to Newcastle, which boasts of lots of coals" , and it is very easy for students to acquire its figurative meaning which is "do something necessary" from "carry coals to Newcastle, which boasts of lots of coals" . The reasoning is as such: Newcastle boasts of coals; if you carry coals to Newcastle, the coals will be more; For Newcastle, increasing some coals brings no advantages. Therefore, *carrying coals to Newcastle* means "do something necessary" . Then, the teacher will give some examples: you are carrying coals to Newcastle, because her family is rich and she is not short of money at all. From the pragmatic perspective, the idiom *carrying coals to Newcastle* is colloquial and is used in daily conversation in most cases. From the cultural perspective, *carrying coals to Newcastle* has no special cultural origin. As illustrated above, the idiom *carrying coals to Newcastle* has been analyzed from the four perspectives: syntactic, semantic, pragmatic, cultural, which is the S-S-P-C model.

"Cold turkey" is another good example. Syntactically, it belongs to the phrase idiom and is subcategorized into the pattern of noun phrase, so the students get to know it acts as grammatical functions of a noun phrase. Semantically, it is difficult for us to deduce its figurative meaning from "cold" and "turkey" . Nevertheless, we can explore its origin from the perspective of culture. Turkey is a very important dish in English family on both Thanksgiving Day and Christmas Day. However, different from chicken on Chinese plates, in English families' eye, turkey is not only ugly but also dull. Imagine what is a cold turkey like? Therefore, if you are called "a turkey", you must be very angry, because you can deduce its meaning is stupid or something from its cultural origin. Pragmatically, it is colloquial and is used in daily conversation. Also, the idiom *cold turkey* has been analyzed under the guide of S-S-P-C model of English idiom acquisition.

The idiom "win laurels" is a third good example. Syntactically analyzed, it is a verb phrase idiom which is mainly used as a predicate component in the sentence. A possessive pronoun can be added in the middle, and "win" can also be replaced by "gain or reap". From a semantic point of view, from the literal meaning of its constituent components "win" and "laurels", it is more difficult to derive its metaphorical meaning. This idiom needs to be explained from a cultural point of view, and this idiom is derived from ancient Greek mythology. Laurel is an ornamental evergreen tree, and laurels refers to a "laurel" made of laurel leaves. The ancient Greeks and Romans made a crown of the leaves of the laurel tree and offered it to outstanding poets or winners of athletic competitions as a reward for their veneration. The fashion spread throughout Europe, and laurels stood for victory, success and distinction. After learning this meaning, we quickly understand the meaning of this idiom, which means "to gain honor, to win prestige". In addition, the teacher can further expand the phrases related to laurels, which also indicate different attitudes towards "honor", and "rest on one's laurels" means "settle for small achievements, do not want to make progress"; "Look to one's laurels" means "be careful to keep honor and be wary of competitors". More examples can be provided to further deepen students' understanding of this idiom, such as "It seems that we can no longer afford to rest on our Laurels" which means "It seems that we can no longer live by eating old books."

Following the S-S-P-C model, the teacher analyzes some idioms as examples. Later on, for every new idiom, students try to analyze from the four perspectives guided by the teacher. From the feedback, students are very interested in this model and are ready to analyze idioms they come across.

9.3.2.3 Results and Discussion

After the teaching experiment was over, we conducted a post-test on Class Two as the teaching experimental class, and Class One as the control class. The test material was another forty idioms randomly chosen from *Oxford Dictionary of Idioms* edited by Judith Siefring. The forty idioms were not included in the subjects' textbooks and different from those in the pre-test. In order to guarantee the materials of pre-test and post-test have similar degrees of difficulties, we chose Class Three as subjects. Those forty-one students from Class Three, who received no teaching experiment, were asked to be tested on the materials of post-test. The scores of the pre-test and the post-test were examined by paired samples statistics and paired samples T-test. The results are shown in Table 9-4 and Table 9-5.

As seen from Table 9-4, average score of pre-test is 31.32, and that of post-test is 33.63. Standard deviation in Pre-test is 12.960, and that in Post-test is 12.545.

Table 9-4 Paired Samples Statistics

	Mean	N	Std. Deviation	Std. Error Mean
Pre-test	31.32	41	12.960	2.024
Post-test	33.63	41	12.545	1.959

The paired samples T-test in Table 9-5 shows that Mean Difference between pre-test and post-test of Class Three is -2.317, and t is -9.54; Two-tailed test is not significant(P=0.346>.05), which demonstrates there are no significant differences between scores of two tests. In other words, the materials of pre-test and post-test have similar degrees of difficulties.

Table 9-5 Paired Samples T-Test

Mean	Std. Deviation	Paired Difference Std. Error Mean	95% Confidence Interval of the Difference		t	df	Sig. (2-tailed)
			Lower	Upper			
-2.317	15.546	2.428	-7.224	2.590	-.954	40	.346

After the material of post-test was examined by paired samples T-test, we conducted the post-test on Class Two as the teaching experiment class, and on Class One as the contrastive class. The method is the same as what the pre-test adopted. In other words, the subjects were expected to translate the English idioms into Chinese. If an idiom was translated correctly, the subject would score 2.5 marks, or else he would score zero. The data was analyzed by SPSS 17.0. The descriptive statistics in Table 9-6 shows that the average score of the control class is 33.42, and that of the teaching experimentd class is 68.51. After the teaching experiment was conducted, the experimental class scored 68.51, much higher than the control class, which scored only 33.42.

Table 9-6 Group Statistics

Class	Groups			
	N	Mean	Std. Deviation	Std. Error Mean
Control Class	43	33.42	14.221	2.169
Experimental Class	40	68.51	11.409	1.740

Independent samples T-test in Table 9-7 shows that F=2.812, and the two-tailed test is significant (P=0<.01), which demonstrates that there are significant differences between scores of the control class and the experimental class after the teaching experiment was conducted.

Table 9-7 Independent Samples T-Test

Class	Levene's Test for Equality of Variances Sig.				
	F	Itself.	t	df	Sig. (2-tailed)
Equal variances assumed	2.812	.097	-12.622	84	.000
Equal variances not assumed			-12.622	80.227	.000

After a semester of experimental teaching, we interviewed some students to investigate the effectiveness of this teaching method. Six students in the experimental class were randomly interviewed and asked two questions: 1. Is it necessary for teachers to adopt this method for idiom teaching? 2. Have you mastered the method of idiom learning?

Interviewee 1: "The teacher explained the idioms very well in this way, and I felt that I had learned a lot."

Interviewee 2: "I now find it very interesting to learn idioms, and I can learn more about British and American culture."

Interviewee 3: "I like the fact that the teacher explains the cultural knowledge behind the idiom."

Interviewee 4: "After class, I also learned to analyze idioms from four perspectives."

Interviewee 5: "After listening to the teacher's explanation, I realized the importance of idioms, and I will learn more idioms in the future."

Interviewee 6: "I like the teacher's use of this method of class, which is very interesting."

After investigation, it was found that students all thought that the teacher took this method well and was conducive to their mastery of the idiom. While learning idioms, it also expands their knowledge and allows them to learn the culture of British and American countries, which is also conducive to improving English proficiency. Secondly, according to the characteristics of idioms, students can better grasp the learning methods of idioms by analyzing idioms from four perspectives. Finally, students' interest in learning English idioms has increased significantly compared to before.

It can be seen that through teaching experiments, the score of idioms of the experimental class is much higher than that of the control class, which indicates that the S-S-P-C English idiom acquisition model is effective for non-English majors.

9.3.3 Conclusion

To sum up, the general aim of the present study is to construct a model of English idiom acquisition suitable for Chinese college students, and the present study have solved the questions put forward in the introduction of the present book. The following conclusions can be drawn.

1) English idiom acquisition is not haphazard. Instead, there is a pattern to follow. Chinese college students need to acquire idioms by following a scientific acquisition model instead of only by rote learning.

2) English idiom acquisition needs to be dealt with from the four perspectives: syntactic, semantic, pragmatic, and cultural, which can be called S-S-P-C model. Syntactic analysis is conducive to students' memorizing idioms' forms and grasp idioms' grammar usages. Semantic analysis helps students acquire figurative meanings of idioms from literal meanings of constituents. Pragmatic perspective makes students develop a pragmatic competence and use idioms appropriately in specified context. Cultural perspective is favorable for students' understanding English idioms in a penetrating way. For comprehending and acquiring idioms comprehensively, students need to integrate the four approaches.

3) The S-S-P-C model is proved to be feasible and efficient. After the model was applied in the teaching experiment, the idiom exams results and the interview with some students show that they improved English idiom acquisition and became interested in English learning.

The present study constructed the S-S-P-C model of English idiom acquisition and applied it in the teaching experiment, which provides insights into an efficient idiom acquisition method different from traditional method characterized with rote learning. Both Chinese college students and their English teachers will be expected to get hints from it. Nevertheless, the present study has still some limitations. For practical reasons, only 40 Chinese college students participated in the teaching experiment for one semester. A larger sample of participants and a longer duration of the teaching experiment would make the S-S-P-C model more valid and reliable.

*The main body of this section has been published with the title of A teaching experiment of Chinese college students' English idiom comprehension in *international Journal of Emerging Technologies in Learning* indexed by EI in June 2017.

10 Conclusion

10.1 Summary

As an integral part of the English language, English idioms play an important role in English as a second language acquisition, especially for college students in China, who often cannot communicate smoothly with English native speakers because of the barrier of idioms. Different from common combinations of two or more words, English idioms have their unique characteristics. Briefly, idioms are conventionalized expressions with figurative or nonliteral meanings, which are not the simple addition of literal meanings of their constituents. Therefore, it is very necessary for Chinese college students to attach great importance to English idiom acquisition and develop suitable and efficient methods in comprehending and acquiring English idioms.

English idioms have distinctive features in terms of pronunciation, structure, semantics, pragmatics, culture, and its variations. Many rhetorical techniques are used in English idioms, such as rhyme, metaphor, personification, antithesis, hyperbole, metonymy, euphemism, and pun. English idioms possess rich pragmatic values and implications. In the process of interpersonal communication, the correct use of English idioms can make language more concise, humorous, and vivid.

Different from common combinations of two or more words, English idioms has their unique syntactic structures. Students should learn to categorize English idioms into different construction patterns. The system of categorization can follow the method of Cowie and his colleagues (1992: xi), that is, English idioms are classified into clause idioms and phrase idioms including several sub-categories. To be specific, clause idioms consist of the five patterns: the pattern of Verb + Complement, Verb + Direct Object, Verb + Direct Object + Complement, Verb+ Indirect Object + Direct Object, and the pattern of Verb + Direct Object + adjunct; phrase idioms consist of another five patterns: the pattern of noun phrase, adjective phrases, prepositional phrase, adverbial phrase, and the pattern of phrase with a repeated or contrastive element. The categorization of idioms can help students put a large amount of disorderly idioms in order and benefit to the student's grasping idioms' grammar usages. In a word, syntactical analysis of idioms can help students memorize idioms' forms and grasp idioms' grammar usages.

Semantic analysis of idioms focuses on idioms' semantic meanings, which are often figurative meanings of idioms as a unit. Figurative meanings are not the simple addition of literal meanings idiom s'constituents. Semantic meanings or figurative meanings are the core of our acquiring and using English idioms. The approach of semantic analysis is helpful for learners' acquiring the idiom's figurative meanings or semantic meanings. English idioms are endowed with three characteristics from the semantic perspective: semantic unity; semantic opacity; semantic peculiarity. Semantic unity means that as an inseparable unit, the figurative meaning of an idiom is not the simple combination of literal meanings of its constituents, but a new meaning brought forth by the construction of idioms. Therefore, traditionally, people insist that the semantic meaning of an English idiom

10 Conclusion

is unpredictable and can be comprehended and acquired only by rote learning. As a matter of fact, there is systematically conceptual relationship between semantic meanings of idioms and their constituents. The nature of semantic unity does not and should not justify that the semantic meaning of an idiom as a unit is unpredictable and can be acquired only by rote learning. Semantic opacity refers to the degree of contributions of individual meanings of the various components of the idioms on the figurative meanings of the idioms or the closeness of ties between literal meanings of idioms and their figurative meanings. Depending on degrees of opacity, idioms can be classified into fully transparent, semi-transparent, and opaque idioms. For idioms with different degrees of opacity, the closeness of tie between literal meanings and figurative meanings varies from each other. The tie is the closest for a transparent idiom, the closer for a semi-transparent idiom, and the loosest or even none for an opaque idiom. Therefore, analyzing literal semantic meanings of an idiom's constituents can help acquire the figurative meaning of the idiom as a unit, especially for transparent idioms and semi-transparent idioms. In fact, this semantic analysis is also suitable for opaque idioms because there is still inner conceptual relationship between figurative meanings of opaque idioms and literal meanings of their constituents. Semantic peculiarity of idioms is represented as two forms: illogical and non-analogical semantically. We cannot speculate semantic meanings of idioms according to our logic, because English idioms have been developed from various ways including historical and social factors besides logic reasoning. Also, we cannot coin semantic meanings of idioms which have similar forms through logical analogy. We can turn to cognitive semantics for analyzing semantic meanings of idioms based on their constituents' literal meanings, because cognitive semantics hold that figurative meanings of idioms have systematical conceptual semantic motivation, which can be found through literal meanings of their constituents.

Besides semantic meanings, English idioms have pragmatic meanings. If learners have not developed pragmatic competence, they cannot use English idioms appropriately even though they have grasped idioms' semantic meanings. The approach of pragmatic perspective can help students acquire idioms' pragmatic meanings, which includes several aspects. Specifically, Chinese students should acquire idioms' stylistic coloring and emotional coloring. Students often make idioms' pragmatic mistakes including pragmalinguisic failure and sociopragmatic failure. The reasons why they make these mistakes are various. With the help of the teachers, students should consciously try to avoid these pragmatic mistakes when using idioms and grasp idioms' stylistic coloring and emotional coloring. Syntactic structure and semantic meaning is not enough for acquiring English idioms, and students have to acquire those idioms' pragmatic meanings so as to avoid pragmatic failures.

The approach of cultural perspective is also necessary for acquiring English idioms. English idioms reflect English native speakers' culture. Some English idioms are endowed with strong cultural coloring. Lack of cultural background of idioms, learners will have difficulties in comprehending and using them and even make native speakers feel abused by the wrong use of them. When acquiring idioms with vivid cultural coloring, students should try to explore cultural background or origins behind them. Familiar with both their own mother language culture and foreign language culture, learners can deepen their comprehension of the target language idioms.

For different kinds of English idioms, college students in China need to integrate the four approaches, and sometimes rely more on some approaches than other approaches. The study has examined English idiom comprehension and acquisition strategies for college students Based on previous empirical research, this study has proposed the M-E-A-N model, the T-R-A-C-E model, and the S-S-P-C model of English idiom acquisition and conducted some teaching experiments, aiming to explore how English as a foreign language learners learn English idioms more effectively.

To sum up, the present study is a comprehensive investigation of English idioms, exploring various aspects of English idioms, including their characteristics, rhetoric, pragmatic analysis, and multidimensional classification. The study has also examined English idiom comprehension and acquisition strategies and constructed three models of English idiom acquisition.

10.2 Theoretical and Pedagogical Implications

The present study has explored and examined various aspects of English idioms, which has both theoretical significance and pedagogical implications.

Specifically, the theoretical contributions mainly include:

1) The present study is helpful in deepening comprehension of idioms' rules and idioms' important role in the system of the English language

2) The present study is helpful in making teachers and students realize that English idiom acquisition has its underlying rules and principles. Idioms can be acquired not by rote learning, but by the syntactic, semantic, pragmatic and cultural analysis.

3) The present study provides a theoretical and pedagogical guide to English idiom acquisition and teaching.

Pedagogically, the present study provides us with the following implications:

1) Instead of only by rote learning, English idiom acquisition can be set about from the four perspectives: syntactic, semantic, pragmatic, cultural.

2) Teachers should instruct students to analyze idioms' syntactic structure and teach students how to induce idioms' figurative meanings from constituents' literal meanings.

3) Teachers need to teach students to discriminate idioms' stylistic and emotional coloring and help them avoid pragmatic mistakes by explain idioms' pragmatic meanings.

4) Teachers can illustrate differences between eastern and western culture and explain origins of some idioms so that students can deepen their comprehension of idioms.

10.3 Limitations and Suggestions for Future Studies

The present study offers a comprehensive examination of English idioms, providing valuable insights into their characteristics, rhetoric, pragmatic analysis, multidimensional classification, comprehension, and acquisition. Both Chinese college students and their English teachers will be expected to get hints from it. Nevertheless, the present study has still some limitations. A comprehensive examination of English idioms is a very great topic, which cannot be thoroughly solved by a single monograph alone of limited length in allowed writing duration. Besides, only 55 Chinese college students participated in the teaching experiment for one semester. A larger sample of participants and a longer duration of the teaching experiment would make the acquisition model more valid and reliable. Therefore, if time permits, future studies will illustrate three English idiom acquisition models in a more penetrating way, and conduct some large-scale teaching experiments. With these issues adequately addressed, we will surely gain more insights into characteristics of English idioms and the rules and principles of English idiom acquisition for Chinese college students.

Bibliography

Austin, J. L. How to do things with words[M]. 2nd ed. Oxford: Clarendon Press, 1975.

Bobrow, S. & Bell, S. On catching on to idiomatic expressions[J]. Memory and Cognition, 1973, 1: 343-346.

Boulenger, V., Hauk, O. & Pulvermuller, F. Grasping ideas with the motor system: Semantic somatotopy in idiom comprehension[J]. Cerebral Cortex, 2009, 19: 1905-1914.

Boers, F. & Demecheleer, M. Measuring the impact of cross-cultural differences on learners' comprehension of imaginable idioms [J]. ELT Journal 55, 2001, 3: 255-262.

Brulé. Children's understanding of ambiguous idioms and conversational perspective-taking[J]. Journal of Experimental Child Psychology, 2012, 112: 437-451.

Cacciari, C. & Tabossi, P. The comprehension of idioms[J]. Journal of Memory and Language, 1988, 27: 668-683.

Caillies, S. &S. Le Sourn-Bissaoui. Idiom comprehension in French children: A cock-and-bull story[J]. European Journal of Developmental Psychology, 2006, 3: 189-206.

Caillies, S. & Butcher, K. Comprehension of idiomatic expressions: Evidence for a new hybrid view[J]. Metaphor and Symbol, 2007, 22: 79-108.

Cain, K., A.S, Towse. & R.S. Knight. The development of idiom comprehension: An investigation of semantic and contextual processing skills[J]. Journal of Experimental Child Psychology, 2009, 102: 280-298.

Chitra Fernando. Idioms and Idiomaticity[M]. Shanghai: Shanghai Foreign language Education Press, 2000.

Constance, Dean Qualls & Joyce L., Harris. Effects of familiarity on idiom comprehension in African American and European American fifth graders[J]. Language, Speech, and Hearing Services in Schools, 1999, 30: 141-151.

Cooper, T.C. Processing of idioms by L2 learners of English[J]. TESOL Quarterly, 1999, 33(2): 233-262.

Crystal, D. The Cambridge Encyclopedia of Language[M]. Cambridge: Cambridge University Press, 1987.

Fernando, C. & Flavell, R. On idioms: Critical views and perspectives[J]. Exeter Linguistic Studies, 1981, 5: 18-48.

Ferando, C. Idioms and Idiomaticity[M]. Oxford: Oxford University Press.

Fraser, B. 1970. Idioms within a transformational grammar[J]. Foundations of Language, 1996, 4: 109-127.

Gibbs, R.W. Spilling the beans on understanding and memory for idioms in context[J]. Memory and Cognition, 1980, 8: 149-156.

Gibbs, R. W. Linguistic factors in children's understanding of idioms[J]. Journal of Child Language, 1987, 14: 569-586.

Gibbs, R.W., Nayak, N.P. & Cutting, C. How to kick the bucket and not decompose: analyzability and idiom processing? [J]. Journal of Memory and Language, 1989, 28: 576-593.

Gibbs, R. W. & Nayak, N. P. Psycholinguistic studies on the syntactic behavior of idioms[J]. Cognitive Psychology, 1989, 21: 100-138.

Gibbs, R.W. Semantic analyzability in children's understanding of idioms[J]. Journal of Speech and Hearing Research, 1991, 34: 613-620.

Gibbs, R. W. What do idioms really mean? [J]. Journal of Memory and Language, 1992, 31: 485-506.

Gibbs, R. W. The poetics of mind[M]. Cambridge: Cambridge University Press, 1994.

Giora, R. On the priority of salient meanings: Studies of literal and figurative language[J]. Journal of Pragmatics, 1999, 31: 919-929.

Halliday, M. A. K. Explorations in the Functions of Language[M]. London: Edward Arnold, 1973.

Hockett, C.F. A course in Modern Linguistics[M], New York: the Macmiian Company, 1958.

Irujo, S. Don't put your leg in your mouth: Transfer in the acquisition of idioms in a second language[J]. TESOL Quarterly, 1986, 20(2): 287-304.

Kerbel, D. A study of idiom comprehension in children with semantic-pragmatic difficulties: Part II. Between-groups results and discussion[J]. International Journal of Language & Communication Disorders, 1998, 33: 23-44.

Kerbel, D., & Grunwell, P. A study of idiom comprehension in children with semantic-pragmatic difficulties. Part I. Task effects on the assessment of idiom comprehension in children[J]. International Journal of Language & Communication Disorders, 1998, 33: 1-22.

Keysar, B. et. al. Swimming against the current: Do idioms reflect conceptual structure[J]. Journal of Pragmatics, 1999, 31:1559-1578.

Lakoff, G. & Johnson, M. Metaphor we live by[M]. Chicago: The University of Chicago Press, 1980.

Leech, G. Principles of Pragmatics[M]. London: Longman, 1983.

Levinson, S. Pragmatics[M]. Cambridge: CUP, 1983.

Makkai, A. Idiom structure in English[M]. The Hague: Mouton, 1972.

Moon, R. Fixed expressions and idioms in English: A corpus-based approach[M]. Oxford: Oxford University Press, 1998.

Nippold, M. A. & T. S. Martin. Idiom interpretation in isolation versus context: a developmental study with adolescents[J]. Journal of speech and Hearing Research, 1989, 32: 59-66.

Nippold, M.A. & J.K., Duthie. Mental imagery and idiom comprehension: A comparison of school-age children and adults[J]. Journal of Speech, Language, and Hearing Research, 2003, 46: 788-799.

Nunberg, G. The pragmatics of reference[M]. Bloomington: Indiana University Linguistics Club, 1978.

Searle, J. R. Expression and meaning[M]. Cambridge: Cambridge University Press, 1979.

Seidl, J & McMordie, W. English idioms and how to use them [M]. Oxford: Oxford University Press,1978.

Sperber, D. & Wilson, D. Relevance: Communication and Cognition (2nd ed)[M]. Oxford: Blackwell, 1986.

Sprenger, S.A., Levelt, W.J.M. & Kempen, G. Lexical access during the production of idiomatic phrases [J]. Journal of Memory and Language, 2006, 54: 161-184.

Strassler, J. Idioms in English: A pragmatic analysis[M]. Tubingen: Gunter Narr, 1982.

Thomas, J. Cross-cultural pragmatic failure[J]. Applied Linguistics, 1983, 4: 91-92.

Titone, D. A. & Connine, C. M. Comprehension of idiomatic expressions: Effects of predictability and literality[J]. Journal of Experimental Psychology: Learning, Memory, and Cognition, 1994, 20: 1126-1138.

Titone, Debra A. & Cynthia M. Connine.On the compositional and non-compositional nature of idiomatic expression[J]. Journal of Pragmatics, 1999, 3: 1655-1674.

Tabossi Patrizia, Rachelie Fanari & Kinou Wolf.Spoken idiom recognition: meaning retrieval and word expectancy[J]. Journal of Psycholinguistics Research, 2005, 34(5): 465-495.

Timothy Reagan, R. The syntax of English idioms: can the dog be put on?[J] Journal of Psycholinguistic Research, 1987, 16(5): 417-441.

Winey, D. A. & Culter, A. The access and processing of idiomatic expressions[J]. Journal of Verbal Learning and Verbal Behavior, 1979, 18: 523-534.

Zhang, hui, Yiming, Yang, Jiexin Gu, & Feng, Ji. ERP correlates of compositionality in Chinese idiom comprehension[J]. Journal of Neurolinguistics, 2013, 26: 89-112.

安静. 浅谈英语习语的翻译方法[J]. 教育教学论坛, 2016, (48): 89-90.

韩舒婷. 浅谈英语习语与英国文化的关系[J]. 戏剧之家, 2017, (1): 255-257.

牟道玉. 茶文化交流在大学英语习语学习中的作用[J]. 福建茶叶, 2017, (03): 241-242.

戴明姝. 英语习语翻译的研究[J]. 英语广场, 2016, (01): 8-10.

常晨光. 英语习语与人际意义[M]. 广州: 中山大学出版社, 2004.

常晨光. 英语习语的人际意义[J]. 外语与外语教学, 2002, 12: 57-63.

陈柏松. 英语习语概论[M]. 武汉: 湖北教育出版社, 1986.

Bibliography

陈慧. 英语习语习得MEAN模式研究[J]. 宁夏大学学报（人文社会科学版），2014，（3）：193-196.

陈慧. 英语习语理解与习得刍议[J]. 广西民族师范学院学报，2014，（5）：85-87.

陈慧. 大学生英语习语习得模式理论及其实践探索[D]. 福建师范大学硕士论文，2014.

陈新仁. 新编语用学教程[M]. 北京：外语教学与研究出版社，2009.

邓炎昌，刘润清. 语言与文化：英汉语言文化对比[M]. 北京：外语教学与研究出版社，1989.

何仁芳. 试论英语习语的分类及特点[J]. 湘潭大学学报（社会科学版），1989，（4）：119-123.

何自然. 语用学概论[M]. 长沙：湖南教育出版社，1988.

何自然，冉永平. 关联理论—认知语用学基础[J]. 现代外语，1998，（3）：92-107.

侯宁海. 英语习语大典[M]. 合肥：中国科学技术大学出版社，2001.

胡文仲. 英语习语与英美文化[M]. 北京：外语教学与研究出版社，2001.

华先发. 英语习语的临时变体[J]. 外语教学与研究，1998，（3）：35-40.

姜望琪. 当代语用学[M]. 北京：北京大学出版社，2011.

蒋磊. 英汉习语的文化观照与对比[M]. 武汉：武汉大学出版社，2000.

金利. 缺失的英文课老外常用习语[M]. 北京：科学出版社，2012.

李珍. 中国大学生对英语习语的理解：语境效应、难易度与二语水平的作用[D]. 湖南大学硕士论文，2011.

廖锡震. 英语成语趣事与幽默会话[M]. 上海：上海译文出版社，

2013.

林维燕. 什么影响我们对英语成语的理解：关于文化差异的母语作用的实验调查报告[J]. 国外外语教学，2003，（3）：34-37.

刘春伟. 英语惯用语终结者[M]. 北京：外文出版社，2010.

刘红丽. 浅谈颜色词在英语和汉语中意义的异同[J]. 哈尔滨职业技术学院学报，2007，（3）：72-73.

刘正光. 惯用语在第二语言习得中的作用与意义研究[J]. 湖南大学学报，2001，（3）：93-97.

刘正光，周红民. 惯用语理解的认知研究[J]. 外语学刊，2002，（2）：7-14.

骆世平. 英语习语研究[M]. 上海：上海外语教育出版社，2006.

闵璇，黄川. 探英语习语揽英美文化[M]. 合肥：安徽科学技术出版社，2011.

彭庆华. 英语习语研究：语用学视角[M]. 北京：社会科学文献出版社，2007.

佘贤君. 惯用语理解的心理机制[J]. 心理学动态，1997，（3）：52-56.

佘贤君，王莉. 惯用语的理解：构造还是提取[J]. 心理科学，1998，（2）：346-384.

佘贤君. 惯用语理解的心理机制[D]. 北京师范大学博士论文，2001.

佘贤君，宋歌，张必隐. 预测性、语义倾向性对惯用语理解的影响[J]. 心理学报，2000，（2）：203-209.

佘贤君，吴建民. 惯用语比喻意义理解的影响因素[J]. 宁波大学学报，2000，（1）：10-13.

佘贤君，吴建民，张必隐. 惯用语比喻意义理解的心理模型[J]. 心理科学，2001，（3）：368-362.

宋志平. 语用翻译与习语误译分析[J]. 外语与外语教学，1998，

(7): 51-53.

粟梅. 大学英语课堂对习语教学的文化导入[D]. 贵州大学硕士论文, 2009.

孙海如, 方如玉. 英语习语来龙去脉[M]. 香港: 商务印书馆, 1988.

唐玉玲. 中国学生英语习语习得模式研究[J]. 江西师范大学（哲学社会科学版）, 2007, 133-137.

唐玲, 苏晓军. 语义分析性、语境和阅读能力对中国EFL学习者英语习语理解的影响[J]. 外国语言文学, 2012, (2): 96-103.

陶岳炼. 英语习语的连接功能[J]. 西安外国语学院学报, 2002, (2): 22-25.

汪家丽. 英语成语故事[M]. 天津: 天津大学出版社, 2013.

汪榕培. 英语词汇学研究[M]. 上海: 上海外语教育出版社, 2000.

汪士彬. 当代英语习语[M]. 北京: 宇航出版社, 1999.

王建勤. 第二语言习得研究[M]. 北京: 商务印书馆, 2009.

王颖. 英语习语整合处理法[M]. 上海: 复旦大学出版社, 2007.

谢华. 熟悉度、透明度和语境对英语学习者理解习语的影响[J]. 解放军外国语学院学报, 2007, (5): 59-64.

闫文培. 现代汉英俗俚语对比研究[M]. 北京: 科学出版社, 2010.

俞珏. 英语习语产出性知识与英语水平的相关性[J]. 安徽师范大学学报（人文社会科学版）, 2011, (3): 369-372.

张雷, 俞理明. 心理类型在中国学生英语习语理解中的作用[J]. 现代外语, 2011, (2): 171-177.

张宁. 英汉习语的文化差异及翻译[J]. 中国翻译, 1999, (3): 23-25.

张培基. 论英语习语的变体[J]. 外国语, 1980, (3): 15-22.

张培基. 英汉翻译教程[M]. 上海: 上海外语教育出版社, 1970.

张若兰. 英汉习语的特点及文化差异[J]. 西安外国语学院学报,

2003，（2）：90-92.

赵朝永. 英语习语：源来如此[M]. 上海：华东理工大学出版社，2010.

郑家顺. 英语谚语5000条[M]. 南京：东南大学出版社，2009.

周英，张淑静. 英语专业学生英语习语加工研究[J]. 解放军外国语学院学报，2011，（3）：46-51.

庄和诚. 英语习语探源[M]. 上海：上海外语教育出版社，2002.

Appendices

I **English Idiom Comprehension From the Syntactic Perspective**

Student number: Class:

Translate the following English idioms into Chinese:

1. turn on
2. hit the books
3. drive someone mad
4. drop someone a line
5. fit someone like a glove
6. white elephant
7. up in the air
8. at the eleventh hour
9. no smoke without fire
10. diamond cut diamond
11. go off
12. burn one's boats
13. call someone names
14. give someone a big hand
15. take something seriously
16. free and easy
17. to pit out
18. behind closed doors
19. through thick and thin
20. hand in hand

21. A piece of cake
22. black horse
23. keep one's word
24. day by day
25. as poor as a rat

II English Idiom Comprehension From the Semantic Perspective

Name: Class:

Translate the following English idioms into Chinese:

1. long time no see
2. run around like a headless fly
3. as old as the hills
4. at large
5. sour grapes
6. at the eleventh hour
7. nothing to write home about
8. get away with
9. look sharp
10. spill the beans
11. face the music
12. a dog's life
13. paint the town red
14. curiosity kills the cat
15. kick the bucket
16. fat chance
17. be all the thumbs
18. as free as a bird
19. red herring
20. covering one's ears while stealing a bell
21. white as a sheet
22. a fine kettle of fish
23. break the ice
24. seeing is believing
25. a dog in the manger

Interview questions:
1.What is your way to learn and acquire English idioms?
2.How do you understand English idioms?
3.What is the problem when you understand English idioms?

III English Idiom Comprehension From the Pragmatic Perspective

Name: Class:

Translate the following English idioms into Chinese:

1. Easy come, easy go
2. Strike while the iron is hot
3. Practice makes perfect
4. Example is better than precept
5. All roads lead to Rome
6. To offer fuel in snowy weather
7. When in Rome.do as the Romans do
8. You are a lucky dog
9. Good helps those who help themselves
10. Spend money like water
11. Out of side, out of mind
12. Live and learn
13. Love me, love my dog
14. Eye for eye
15. Let the cat out of the bag
16. White lie
17. No pains, no gains
18. a piece of cake
19. Look before you leap
20. Kill the time
21. Go dutch
22. Curiosity kills the cat
23. like father, like son
24. White as a sheet
25. Practice makes effect

Interview questions:
1. How do you learn idioms in your daily life?
2. What's your attitude towards idioms?
3. Do you usually use the idioms in your daily life?

IV English Idiom Comprehension From the Cultural Perspective

Materials for Pre-test

student number:　　　　　Class:

Choose the best answer:

1. At the eleventh hour
   A. at the last minute
   B. At eleven o' clock
   C. Other

2. last supper
   A. Last meal
   B. The Last Supper
   C. Other

3. Judas kiss
   A. Mouth honey belly sword
   B. God's Kiss
   C. Other

4. go for it
   A. Strive for
   B. Do
   C. Other

5. in the long run
   A. During long-distance running
   B. In the long run
   C. Other

6. fly a kite
   A. Kite flying
   B. Tempting public opinion or public opinion
   C. Other

7. put an ear to the ground
   A. Ear fell to the ground
   B. Proceed with caution
   C. Other
8. in all weathers
   A. Whenever
   B. Rain or shine
   C. Other
9. in hot water
   A. In dire straits
   B. in water which is hot
   C. Other
10. a dark horse
    A. A dark horse
    B. Surprise
    C. Other
11. love me love my dog
    A. Love me and my dog
    B. Love one thing on account of another
    C. Other
12. as cute as a bug
    A. same as black hole
    B. Lovely
    C. Other
13. bed of roses
    A. Rose bed
    B. hot bed
    C. Other

14. a hot potato
    A. Tricky things
    B. a potato which is hot
    C. Other
15. gild the lily
    A. pure as a lily
    B. draw a snake and add feet to it
    C. Other
16. like a house on fire
    A. anxious
    B. Rapid
    C. Other
17. bottom line
    A. intolerable range
    B. Underline
    C. Other
18. make hay
    A. Sunbathing
    B. Seize the moment
    C. Other
19. break a leg
    A. broken leg
    B. Good luck
    C. Other
20. all thumbs
    A. Clumsiness
    B. Awesome
    C. Other

21. Be all ears
    A. beware of eavesdroppers
    B. Listen to
    C. Other
22. loose cannon
    A. loss of control
    B. I go my own way
    C. Other
23. top gun
    A. Superior gun
    B. Outstanding person
    C. Other
24. baby kisser
    A. Beloved
    B. Sleek politician
    C. Other
25. hit the mark
    A. hit target
    B. grades decreased by
    C. Other
26. jam tomorrow
    A. doomsday
    B. never deliver on a promise
    C. Other
27. a sorry sight
    A. miserable
    B. can't bear to look directly at
    C. Other

28. pandora' box
    A. pandora's Box
    B. the source of sin
    C. Other
29. a dog in the manger
    A. occupy the pit and do not
    B. Dog jumps off the wall
    C. Other
30. Lion's share
    A. largest share
    B. share
    C. Other

V English Idiom Comprehension From the Cultural Perspective

Materials for Post-test

Student number:　　　　　　Class:

Choose the best answer:

1. Adam's Apple

    A. larynx

    B. the apple of a person called Adam

    C. other

2. clean hands

    A. Integrity

    B. hand washing

    C. other

3. the apple of one's eye

    A. someone's most precious things

    B. the eye of God

    C. other

4. jump the gun

    A. Premature action

    B. skip gun

    C. other

5. pull one's weight

    A. weight loss

    B. Go all out

    C. other

6. break the ice

    A. break the ice into pieces

    B. start further discussion

    C. other

7. blood is thicker than water

   A. People who are related by blood should be closer to each other than those who are not related by blood

   B. compared with water. blood is thicker

   C. other

8. in the wind

   A. greeting the wind

   B. upcoming

   C. other

9. a little bird told me

   A. pigeon message

   B. someone told me privately

   C. other

10. fish in troubled waters

   A. gain advantage in a confused situation

   B. try to catch fishes in dirty water

   C. other

11. the black sheep

   A. some black sheep

   B. horse that spoils the whole herd

   C. other

12. in hot water

   A. In dire straits

   B. in water which is hot

   C. Other

13. couch potato

   A. people who like to laze on the couch and watch TV

   B. potato on the sofa

C. other
14. sour grapes
    A. grapes which are sour
    B. unattainable things
    C. other
15. beat around the bush
    A. flee here and there
    B. hint obliquely
    C. other
16. worth one's salt
    A. be as stubborn as a mule
    B. Competent
    C. other
17. strike it rich
    A. sudden windfall
    B. discover mineral
    C. other
18. get the sack
    A. carry a sack
    B. dismiss sb. from his job
    C. other
19. pay through the nose
    A. cost a lot
    B. lead by the nose
    C. other
20. wet behind the ears
    A. be brainless
    B. be young and inexperienced

C. other
21. bite your tongue
    A. silence
    B. repeat other people's words like a parrot
    C. other
22. dry run
    A. run without drinking water
    B. rehearsal
    C. other
23. field day
    A. exciting times
    B. picnic day
    C. other
24. hot seat
    A. a seat which is hot
    B. embarrassing situation
    C. other
25. as pure as the driven snow
    A. pure and innocent
    B. Snowy
    C. other
26. bag and baggage
    A. all property of a person
    B. all bags
    C. other
27. heart's content
    A. do something as much as you want
    B. tolerance

C. other
28. Helen of Troy
   A. serious disasters brought about by the most beloved person (thing)
   B. the love of my heart
   C. other
29. swan song
   A. last words written before death
   B. a person's final public performance before retirement
   C. other
30. under the rose
   A. the literal meaning. i.e.. under the rose instead of on top of the rose
   B. in confidence
   C. other

VI   Construction of S-S-P-C Model of English Idiom Acquisition

Materials for Pre-test

Name: Class:

Translate the following English idioms into Chinese:

1. like a fish out of water
2. Travelling is just his cup of tea.
3. That's another cup of tea.
4. He's very unpleasant cup of tea.
5. clever dog
6. cat and dog life
7. Sam is a friend you can always depend on. rain or shine.
8. He saved a little money for a rainy day.
9. It's a real bread and butter satellite.
10. They asked some bread and butter questions.
11. She is still a bread and butter miss.
12. a storm in a tea cup
13. free and easy
14. pull the weight
15. as cool as a cucumber
16. kill two birds with one stone
17. castle in the air
18. go through fire and water
19. feel like a million dollars
20. fall on deaf ears
21. find fault with
22. burn one's boat
23. but me no buts
24. be left in the cold

25. at be bottom of one's heart
26. at sixes and sevens
27. go from bad to worse
28. never say die
29. pull one's leg
30. say eye to eye with
31. fall head over in love
32. ten to ten
33. It's not my day.
34. day in, day out
35. earn one's salt
36. not worth a bean
37. an elephant's memory
38. turn one's back on sb. /sth.
39. wolf food down
40. count sheep

VII   Construction of S-S-P-C Model of Acquisition

Materials for Post-test

Name: Class:

Translate the following English idioms into Chinese:

1. outsmart oneself
2. think twice before you leap
3. rain cats and dogs
4. a black day for someone
5. once bitten. twice shy
6. every dog has its day
7. break the ice
8. have nine lives
9. love me love my dog
10. busy as a bee
11. a wolf in sheep's clothing
12. hot potato
13. the black sheep of the family
14. let the cat out of the bag
15. A friend in need is a friend indeed
17. have no choice
18. a piece of cake
19. worth one's salt
20. once in a blue moon
21. drink like a fish
22. wash one's hands of
23. make yourself at home
24. no ifs. ands or buts
25. bury one's head in the sand

26. come to an end
27. have no time for something
28. wet behind the ears
29. break one's back
30. be a black mood
31. white elephant
32. spill the beans
33. make sb.'s blood boil
34. a bad apple
35. fat cat
36. rat race
37. search me
38. Yes. that was it. I had it now. it was all coming back to me
39. You needn't think you're going to behave in that way. I won't have it
40. I've had it! Let's stop and rest